My Love Affair With Life

. . . a memoir . . .

by

Judy Gascoyne

My Love Affair With Life

. . . a memoir . . .

by

Judy Gascoyne

First Published by Island Books, Isle of Wight

Copyright © 2002 by Judy Gascoyne

ISBN 1898 198 17 9

British LIbrary Catalogue in Publishing Data

A catalogue record for this book is available from the British Library

Designed by Percy Westwood, and produced by con**text**, Isle of Wight

Authors Note

In this book I have referred to my - possibly flawed - memory and my diary notes. Where I express an opinion, it is just that: my opinion. I have met many wonderful people in my life, especially in the last twenty years. They exist within this book as reflected within my eyes, and the reflection may not be what they expect. I wish no-one any harm, and if any minor offence has been caused I hereby apologise.

I must thank Roger Scott, my dear friend, for proof-reading my text, thanks, Roger.

I have enjoyed my life so far as you will see within this book, and hope that some enjoyment may accrue to the reader, certainly a view into the misty world of poets!

At David's funeral, his poem *Lines* was read as his coffin was brought in to the church. I include it here:

Lines

So much to tell: so measurelessly more
Than this poor rusting pen could ever dare
To try to scratch a hint of . . . Words are marks
That flicker through men's minds like quick black dust;
That falling, finally obliterate the faint
Glow their speech emanates. Too soon all sparks
Of vivid meaning are extinguished by
The saturated wadding of Man's tongue . . .
And yet, I lie, I lie:
Can even Omega discount
The startling miracle of human song?

David Gascoyne

Table of Contents

Dedication

I would like to dedicate these memoirs to my husband, David Gascoyne.
Being married to a poet and writer is an education in itself, so when I told him
that I wanted to write my autobiography, he was most encouraging and said,
Get on with it then!

It wasn't until I tried to do it that I realised what dedication is needed, and that
you must stick to it every day. I felt guilty of the many times when I secretly
thought that David was being lazy when he suffered from weeks of writer's
block.

Well, I did get on with it - sometimes it was easy, and sometimes I felt
inadequate, but my motto has always been *'Nothing is impossible'* so I plodded
on with it.

The title came to me because years ago, when I was at a very low ebb, a
psychiatrist at Whitecroft Mental Hospital told me I would soon get over it
'because I had a sort of *love affair with life.'*

Judy Gascoyne, April 2001

Early Years

One day I'll write my memoirs. I've said this so often, and now I'm actually starting on them. It's quite a therapeutic thing to do, and not really a waste of time because it may be of interest to my children and grandchildren. I would love to have known about the lives of my grandparents, but there is no-one I can ask about them now.

I've started now in 1998, and I hope to get it finished as a little present to myself, and for anyone else who may be interested, by the year 2000.

My birth at the End Farm, Marlow, Bucks on February 1st 1922, has been well recorded in my father's diary, but I enjoy embellishing it by the story he told me himself. Apparently, after a fairly difficult home-birth, the doctor told my father, 'Your wife is fine, but I'm afraid that your daughter has failed to breathe.' Having two sons, my father wanted a daughter and he was heart-broken. Nothing daunted, he told me that he rushed upstairs, took me from under the bed and resuscitated me! My father was a farmer and I've often thought that he did this because he'd revived animals when they were born supposedly dead. I also think that because of this traumatic birth, I had a great bond with my father and he, in return, spoilt me shamelessly. Perhaps this is why I've grown up with the feeling that everyone is kind, and that anything I want will be given to me.

As people don't often listen when you talk to them, I think it's important to write things down - and this is why I'm having some thoughts about my dear father, Guy.

*   *   *   *

He was very handsome in a rugged sort of way, with deep blue eyes and a beautiful voice. He was the second son of William Tyler, a famous English sculptor; his mother was a very distinguished lady called Isabella whose family came from the court of Spain. Apart from a very beautiful portrait of her (which makes me believe she was an enchanting person) I know very little of her - and now there is no one to ask.

This is why I want to write about Guy Tyler — just a short pen portrait, so that my grandchildren and others may know what he was like.

My two elder children knew and loved him. He died in 1966, but I love thinking about him and the times we had together. Above all, he always made me feel so confident and happy. His love for me was such a joy; when I read his diaries (which he kept religiously all his life) I am deeply touched by his references to me.

I owe him a great deal. His example has inspired me to keep a diary every day now for twenty years, and at other special times in my life: 1937, 1940, 1944, 1955, 1966, 1974, for example.

I loved the way Guy set about doing things: so methodically, and yet with such a sense of enjoyment. Every evening after working very hard on the farm, he would change out of his working clothes, and appear elegantly at six, for a sherry. When I was really young, we used to dance together to Henry Hall's band on the radio. I used to stand on his feet to get the rhythm. Later when I was older, I used to share a drink with him, and we would talk or read poetry until it was time for supper.

Dear Guy was always so patient with my many unsuitable boyfriends! But when he liked them, I knew I was on to someone good; he was very gentle with them. A few years ago, I met up with a boy I hadn't seen for forty years and whom I had loved very much. His words about my father touched me deeply. He told me that he'd modelled his life on my father, and that he admired him more than anyone he had ever met.

Perhaps his strange upbringing and later tough life taught Guy to be brave and not fuss over things. In brief, he was the son of a sculptor and had no formal education - he had his upbringing in the rich houses of foreign royalty where his father was sculpting statues of the wealthy. A tutor was sometimes provided. During their stay on Capri, the family all learnt to swim like fishes, and talk like natives.

I'm never quite sure why, but at the age of eighteen, my father decided to become a Royal Canadian Mounted Policeman. This must have been a challenging time; I loved hearing stories about it. He used to ride from outpost to outpost in freezing conditions, coping with all sorts of difficult situations. Perhaps that's why he loved the poetry of Robert Service so much.

After a few strenuous years in the bitter cold, he became a rubber planter in Kuala Lumpur, Malaysia. That's where he met my mother, who was making a pilgrimage to her fiancé's grave in Singapore, He admired her instantly, and followed her back to England to propose. When they met this handsome and distinguished man, her five sisters were very envious.

The marriage on January 3rd, 1915, was a quiet affair because it was also a National Day of Prayer for the war in all the churches. I came on the scene in 1922, on February 1st, and was born at the farm at Marlow which my father had bought. He was 80% disabled from a war wound in his head, and was advised to do something simple - not that farming is ever simple or easy, but my many boyfriends enjoyed helping him out.

During his war service, my father was awarded the Military Cross and Bar for bravery, but he never boasted about it.

The farm was an idyllic place for my two brothers and me. It was up on a hill overlooking Marlow, and my favourite moments were sitting on the verandah watching the lights of the town gradually switching on. Sometimes a huge moon would rise over the enormous cherry tree. I have travelled a lot over the past eighteen years with my poet husband, but seldom have I seen anything so poetic or beautiful.

All through my years of growing up, my father was so supportive and understanding. When I was fat and spotty, and very plain, he always boosted my morale. When a young teenager and a wicked flirt, I felt like a princess because I knew he would select the right partner for me. One evening when I was seventeen, I asked him if he thought I would get married to the right man. 'Surely as night follows day', he answered - and he was right (although in the end I married two *right men* - but that's another story). I felt very proud walking up the aisle for my first marriage in 1945.1 wish, too, that my father could have known my second husband, David Gascoyne; I know they would have liked one another.

One of the happiest memories of my father was when Sue, my second child, was born at his house in Marlow in May. Guy's birthday was in May too, and he was thrilled when was Sue was born - and so was I.

When we eventually found the house of our dreams at Yarmouth on the Isle of Wight, my father used to come and stay with us. His visits were always memorable because he was so relaxed and appreciative. We spent long days by the sea when the children were small, and he once paid me a compliment which has lived with me always: 'Your children all love each other', he would say, 'and that is rare'. Nowadays with the family all in their forties, his words have proved true: they are all so loving and supportive of one another.

Guy's death was many years ago now. It was swift and sudden - just as he would have wished. He was mowing the lawn, awaiting the arrival of my brother and children for a little holiday. A heart-attack overtook him and he died instantly.

He had often talked to me of death. 'I want to die quickly', he always said. 'I couldn't bear to be in a home, or to have a lingering death in hospital'.

His funeral in the Catholic Church at Marlow was very moving. All the family were there of course, and a collection of beautiful young people - many actually in tears. I had to be brave and support them.

Now that my father is no longer with me to give me comfort and advice, I take great joy in writing these words about him. These days the rich and famous get really good obituaries written for them in all the major papers. I wish there could have been one worthy of my father. — Captain Guy Tyler MC, born 1884, married 1915, three children, died Marlow 1966.

*   *   *   *

My childhood was pleasant. It was good to live on a farm which overlooked Marlow and had miles of unspoilt views. My brothers, who I adored, were sent off to Prep School at quite a tender age, while I was left at home to boss everyone about. I have a vivid memory of when my mother got the better of me - she had taken me to Marlow in my pushchair, and allowed me to walk a little. However, time was passing and she wanted me to return to my pushchair so that we could return home quickly. I refused, so my mother asked a passing policeman to order me into it. That quite scared me, although he only said, 'Get into your pushchair little girl'. I think I've kept a healthy respect for the police since that time!

When I was six, the milkman's daughter, Miss Smith, came to teach me every morning. I enjoyed this and I can still recall the joy I felt when I could read *The Little Red Hen* all by myself. My cousin Betty came to live with us during term time, and she joined in the lessons with me. I recall, with shame, how I bossed her about and dared her to scribble on her copy book to annoy Miss Smith. She was easily influenced and she brought out the worst in my bossy nature.

In those days middle class children didn't often go to the State schools. It was either a boarding school or home education. By the time I was thirteen, even my father was finding me a bit of a trial, so it was decided that I should go as a weekly boarder to Lynton House School at Maidenhead.

I enjoyed this experience more than I expected, and had the best of both worlds. Luckily I kept a diary for the two years I was at school, so I can recall quite accurately what it was like. My father drove me in the car on Monday morning, and I stayed at school until Friday afternoon.

Strangely enough, the school-work came quite easily, except for maths which Miss Smith hadn't really touched on. French, English and History interested me very much. Our English teacher gave me my great love of Shakespeare and poetry, and my French teacher made me write out all the verbs in every tense as a punishment for talking in class. So that has stood me in good stead for teaching French, which I still do now.

The usual school things happened. Disastrous midnight feasts in the dormitory, pashes on older girls and then when I was fifteen they had pashes on me. I was nearly expelled for encouraging boys to come and whisper to us at night from the next-door house! My father fetched me faithfully at 4 pm every Friday and took me out to tea and then to a cinema. I must have seen every film that ever came out in the thirties, and I loved them. When we started working for our school certificate, the Headmistress wrote to my father and said I must become a full boarder to work for the exams. When I explained to him that I wouldn't be able to stand that, he agreed. Because of that I've never had to work for school exams in my life. Two things I really enjoyed at school were tennis and elocution. The latter introduced me to poetry of all kinds, and I did take exams for that up to the silver medal. At fifteen it was decided that I'd had enough of school, so I left. Two years was quite enough for me. Plans were then made for me to be *finished off* at a Swiss Finishing School. Luckily, there were hints of a war brewing, and my father didn't want me to risk it. So, before the real war started, I went once a week to a very expensive school in London, where I learned how to speak Shakespeare quite well, and to learn lots of it by heart. I was also enjoying the fun of flirting and the social life that the thirties offered for the young and spoilt. I can recall staying at huge country houses, where one had to dress for dinner and be waited on by servants. The tennis parties and dances were very grand too.

An amazing holiday in Klosters given me by my rich uncle was the highlight of a Christmas when I was sixteen. I had a really wonderful time. The skiing came quite easily to me. The boys were very attractive undergraduates, and I much enjoyed the dancing and flirting in the evenings. During the year of 1939 I went to many grand dances, and was a semi-Deb, not being old enough or rich enough to be a real one.

On September 3rd 1939, we were all woken up from our dream world when the war was announced by Neville Chamberlain one fine Sunday morning. Most people of my age can recall exactly what they were doing at that moment. I was sitting on the veranda at the farm with my mother and father. When the Air Raid siren sounded at the end of the announcement, it was quite a shock to us all. To me it seemed like a bad dream. Nothing much happened after that for the first few weeks, and as I didn't keep a diary that year, I'm not too clear about my memories of nearly sixty years ago.

I did a bit of evacuee work and I was astounded by the number of people who made excuses about taking in children when the air raids started. I felt very unsettled. A 'phone call from Mrs Waterhouse Jones early in 1940 cheered me up. She had started a private school in Marlow with her daughter, and they now had more pupils than they could cope with. 'Would I like to come and help out every morning with the new 5 year olds in the entrance class?' she asked. The idea pleased me very much, and in January 1940 I started to work at Dial Close School in Marlow. The children were intelligent and easy to teach, and it wasn't long before I was asked to go full time. The job was exactly what I wanted, and I was thrilled when the children enjoyed the lessons as much as I did. I devised my own method of reading, writing and spelling, and it gives me much satisfaction that now, fifty-eight years on, I'm still having success with the pupils who come to me privately.

In those days you kept your own class all the time, and so they all stayed with me for four years. In 1944 I was called up to be a Signalwoman on the GAR. The teaching of these children at Marlow is very much on my mind at this moment, because their school had its first reunion this year. I was immensely touched and surprised to meet so many of my old pupils, all now in their sixties, and we were able to recall all the fun we had together. They were a bright lot, and many of them have done really well. In fact, this reunion in June of this year, 1998, was one of the happiest events in my happy life. I think its because of its success that I have started to write these memoirs.

The call-up in 1944 came as quite a nasty surprise! I had imagined that helping my father, before and after school, on the farm and teaching all day could be regarded as a reserved occupation. I appealed against the call-up, but the panel of ladies turned me down.

I have noticed throughout my life that, when anything bad happens, something better than you'd ever hoped for takes its place. Many people agree with me over this. So, in spite of making a great deal of fuss about leaving my children and the school job, I found the job in the Signal Box at Marlow to be very much to my liking, and it taught me quite a few things too. To start with, it was quite a challenge. The War Office had decided to train women to take over Signal Boxes so that the men could be released for heavier tasks. There weren't many of us but at Marlow three girls were taken on for the job of manning the Box in shifts. First we had to learn all the tricky bits of signalling at Reading Station with an Inspector Meade. We travelled free on the trains, and we had to learn a lot. I was determined to learn quickly because I fancied taking on the Signal Box alone as soon as possible. The actual learning about how the Box worked was difficult because Mr Morgan wasn't really eager to teach us and leave his precious Box for another job. We would have to spend 8 hours alone with him listening to his Welsh jokes and trying to pick up the hang of it all. I used to bribe him shamelessly with farm eggs and greengages! Eventually it was time for an Inspector to watch me in the Box, and decide if I was fit to 'pass out' before three Paddington Signal Inspectors. I was greatly pleased when that day came, and I was declared to be a GAR Signalwoman 2nd Class, with a uniform, a union badge and £5.10s a week for a wage. An enormous increase from my teaching wage of 30/-. If I go into more details about this than I should, its because now in my 70s I am regularly asked to give talks about it to all the Island organisations. They seem really fascinated by it all, and perhaps we should all write our War Work memories in detail.

My war work lasted until I married on July 7th 1945. I had a very happy wedding day and the reception for about 200 people was at our farm. In spite of a little opposition, I married Michael Lewis when he was only a Veterinary student. His father, Strafford Lewis, an eminent psychiatrist and Superintendent at St Bernard's Hospital, decided that Michael would probably pass his exams better if he married first, so he offered us £4 a week to live on. We gladly accepted this as, in those days, it was quite a fortune. My rich uncle sent us £200 for a honeymoon, so we were 'up and away'. I recall a funny incident which occurred on the 'Honeymoon Express', as they used to call it, on our journey with the GAR from Paddington to Penzance. I had become very friendly with all the other Signalmen when I worked the Marlow Box. Somehow they found out which train I'd be on, and I soon discovered that there was a Signalman waving to us from every box as we went on our way. Some of them had even put up a sign *Good luck Judy.* This made me feel quite like the Queen, even though it was a tiring journey! I have enduring memories of my time with the GAR, and the friendliness of all the workers. I was able to send off a Troop train non-stop to the coast on D-Day.

The honeymoon at a private hotel on the Herford River was enjoyable. The weather was typical, mostly wet and windy. In the evenings all the guests were at one big table for supper, then we all played pencil and paper games, which I organised, or else we had a piano recital from the owner's wife who was a concert pianist.

At the end of two weeks, we returned to a cottage on my father's farm to stay until Michael had to return to the Veterinary College at Streamlet-on-Thames. We stayed in a bed and breakfast there which wasn't too special. I was pregnant by then and suffering the early stages of morning sickness. I enjoyed meeting the other students and being at the college. On June 16th 1946 I gave birth to a son at a Nursing Home in Maidenhead. I had read Dr Grantley Dick Reid's book about painless childbirth, and while I was in labour I felt like tearing up the whole book! However, Kevin was born after eight long hours, weighing about 9 lb. In those days it was customary to stay at least two weeks in bed after a birth. I hated the Nursing Home and wrote to my doctor saying I must be allowed home to my farm or my milk would turn sour!

As soon as possible I rejoined Michael at the College in Streamlet. We managed to have really nice digs by then. A huge house by the river owned by a rather eccentric lady was put at the disposal of the Veterinary students. We were given the very elegant drawing room with large French windows. It made an excellent bed-sitter. The kitchen was rather far away, and so was the bathroom, but we managed well. I was glad of all the help given me by the girl veterinary students. They thought Kevin was a gorgeous baby and he loved their attentions. While we were there Michael qualified as a Vet, and there was much rejoicing.

The first job Michael took was in Ryde in the Isle of Wight. We lived above Young's the Electricians in the High Street. Kevin was a good baby and all through the summer I was on the beach with him every day. We arrived there in January 1947 which was one of the coldest winters on record, and there was no coal to be had so our flat was freezing. In retrospect I think I was very lonely. Michael was overworked and on call day and night. The Vet's wife was very neurotic and she didn't help me much. I wasn't able to take a job because of Kevin. Eventually we decided to leave and I went back to Marlow to have my daughter, Sue, at my parents' house. This couldn't have been a better arrangement. I was able to see all my old friends, and entertain Kevin with much enjoyment. On May 6th 1948 Sue was born on a beautiful May evening. It all happened so peacefully and easily that when she was actually born I had to say to the midwife, who was reading the Tatler, 'Excuse me, but I think my baby has been born!' The family were quite thrilled about it all, and so was I. However, my mother said it would be better if Kevin could have a two week holiday with his other grandmother, and off he went quite happily. Michael had a new job in Wells in Somerset, and I was anxious to join him down there. On Kevin's second birthday, and with Sue about six weeks old, we travelled in a furniture van with some of our accumulated furniture. It was an exciting journey with many stops at 'lorry drop-ins' which Kevin enjoyed, and the van driver dropped us off at a farmhouse near Wells.

There life was rather primitive and difficult. No running water in the scullery kitchen, so washing nappies for Sue was difficult, and only a little oil stove for cooking. Somehow we managed until we moved into the attic of the Vet's house in Wells. I like writing about some of the hardships we went through so that I can appreciate life now.

When we moved from the farmhouse, to an attic in the Vet's house in Wells, life wasn't much easier there. The Vet and his wife went on holiday and I was responsible for all the veterinary 'phone calls. Quite a task because it entailed running down four flights of stairs and having to leave Sue aged 4 months, and Kevin aged 2½ to their own devices. However, we survived for about 6 months in that job. I became hysterical one day and Michael realised that I'd had enough.

With no job or money, we accepted the hospitality of Michael's mother. After the ghastly trauma of her divorce from Dr Lewis, she was living peacefully in Ealing. Dorothy couldn't have been a better mother-in-law: she was gentle and wise, and quietly efficient. She came to my rescue many times during my marriage. While Michael was applying for jobs I found myself one. I passed by a boys' school where there was a notice: *Teacher needed urgently.* I went to see the Headmaster. He didn't tell me that the need was because the previous teacher was suffering from a nervous breakdown trying to control a class where they had put all the difficult teenagers. I soon discovered the trouble and shamelessly used my youth and charm to seduce the two ringleaders. Mostly I made them into teams against each other, and as they wanted to win the quizzes I set, peace reigned. The result was a glowing reference when I eventually had to leave! A job had been found in Stratford-upon-Avon, with a house attached, so life was getting easier.

To live in Stratford-upon-Avon is a real privilege, not only because of the grand theatre where the best actors in the world played Shakespeare every night, but there were also wonderful poetry readings every week with the likes of Sybil Thorndike, Peggy Ashcroft and John Gielgud. Also, it was a pleasant, friendly town. While I was there I was very busy, firstly becoming an agent for Roland Brown, the Labour Party candidate. We fought a fierce, but obviously losing, battle against John Profumo. Secondly, we decided to have two more children. My Jenny was born six weeks early at home. It was another easy birth and she was a magical baby. Kevin and Sue were very helpful, and got themselves off to school on their own. Eighteen months later Milo arrived, a bit late but very welcome, with the ease of a home birth again.

On top of all this, we had many friends wanting to stay in our tiny house, mostly because of the Royal Shakespeare Theatre. Tickets were hard to come by and it often meant queuing for hours.

The cause of our leaving Stratford was because of a hepatitis virus which attacked me, and later Michael. For the six weeks when I was ill I really quite wished to die. My doctor was so worried that he cut short his holiday in order to attend to me. I wasn't able to rest much with four children, and the youngest insisted on being breastfed, although he was already nine months old.

I must make some comments about my beautiful house Westport:

*   *   *   *

When Michael caught hepatitis from me it was a gloomy time because he was very ill too and he didn't wish to be disturbed. While pondering over his illness he hatched a plan to have a holiday to recover on the Isle of Wight. Whilst there he discovered that there seemed to be only one Vet to attend to all the Island animals, and he proposed to set up practice there. I wasn't all that keen on the idea, but I realised that it might be a good move. We borrowed £1,000 from Michael's two aunts, and his father too. Estate Agents sent us lists of available houses, and we set our hearts on a doctor's house in Yarmouth with a large walled garden near the sea . The price was £4,000 and we managed to get them to accept £3,500. The last few weeks at Stratford-upon-Avon were quite poignant: all Michael's clients gave him presents. I had to say goodbye to the children where I had been teaching once a week, and at a farewell party my doctor confessed that he had been in love with me ever since I'd arrived at his surgery with ear ache! All very surprising. Our furniture went ahead of us and we spent the night with dear friends, the Harmers, who gave us a bottle of champagne to open on our arrival.

It was a bright April day in 1956 when we arrived in Yarmouth, and I saw the house for the first time. Like Martin Luther King, I also had had a dream! A more selfish one than his it's true, but while living in Stratford on Avon with four small children, I used to imagine my perfect house by the sea. We were soon unpacked and sorted out. Having a surgery and a waiting room opening onto a side lane was a real boon for the start of the Veterinary Practice.

Although I had never seen Westport, I had formed a clear picture of what it would be like. I wasn't disappointed! We arrived about 2 pm on a sunny, windy, spring day. Westport was exactly the house of my dreams. A large, well-built brick house with a beautiful wide door to welcome us into a large hall and spacious rooms. The garden was big and lovely too, and there was a nice brick wall all around it. There were many fruit trees in blossom and daffodils everywhere.

When the furniture arrived an hour later, we had all decided exactly where everything was to go. After our tiny house in Stratford it was good to have plenty of room for all our treasures. I gathered bunches of daffodils to give to the removal men. I expect they would have preferred money, but we had hardly any to spare!

In those days no advertising for veterinary services was allowed, so we had to put up our little brass plate and hope for the best. Yarmouth is a very friendly town, and they welcomed us warmly, saying they were pleased to have a Vet on the spot. They were very generous when I went shopping: the fishmonger saved me all his left-overs saying: 'These are for your poor sick pussy-cats'. Little did he know that I used them for many good fish pies for us all. Also, when I returned from the greengrocers, I used to find that my friend from the shop had been more than generous in filling my shopping bags with fruit and vegetables. Two nice things happened, the local solicitor called and we opened our precious bottle of champagne given us by dear friends in Stratford, and my uncle, Lord Parmoor came for the day while we were still in a bit of a muddle. The next day he sent us £200 *to get us started*. That was a really kind gesture and it was such a help.

Nevertheless, the surgeries were often empty, but that gave Michael plenty of time to sort out the house and garden. When the summer arrived we spent much time at Love Shore which was five minutes from the house. Also many visitors wanted to come over to the Island.

Soon, word went round that the new vet was good. At first only the local people and visitors tried us, but later the farmers cautiously decided to call us out. Someone always had to be on duty for the 'phone, but I was always glad of an excuse not to leave our beautiful house and garden.

Another thing happened when we arrived at Westport. We needed more furniture for all the big rooms after our tiny 'semi' in Stratford. So off I went to the local furniture auction. There, Steve Ross, the auctioneer, began to notice me and he was constantly knocking things down to me for a shilling or two! We became friends and I soon met his charming wife, Brenda, and all their children who were the same age as ours. I was asked if I would like to be the Liberal Candidate for the Island. I refused politely but gave them Steve's address. And so I helped him fight two elections, and the third one we got him in as our Island MP. It was a magic moment for all of us. On television he made amusing remarks that I was to blame for all of it, but I loved Steve and his family dearly. It was good that he was made Lord Ross of Newport, an award he richly deserved. Sadly he died far too young from a heart attack in the early nineties.

Soon the practice became quite busy and Michael was able to employ help. Christine Carver used to arrive with her two small children, and I looked after them while she helped Michael. A big crisis happened to me on our arrival for our first Christmas. I discovered a lump in my breast. The Consultant surgeon wanted to remove the whole breast just at Christmas time. I implored him to wait, but he said, 'If you were my wife I'd operate this afternoon'. The day the summons came, just a week before Christmas, the lump had disappeared. We had the best Christmas of our lives, no time for preparations - just rejoicing. For the next three years I collected money for cancer research and became well-known for scouring all the Yarmouth pubs with my tins. So something good came out of that after all.

Wanting to give something back for the kindness I had received, I started a Youth Club in Yarmouth and became Secretary for the Carnival. I also went wholeheartedly into working for charities - Cancer Research, Mind Campaign - and we started a Cheshire Home on the Island. Westport was a perfect place to invite people for committee meetings and we always enjoyed the laughter and chat. Because of the veterinary calls the house could never be left empty. Two very special events were a garden party in aid of the Cheshire Home, and my daughter Sue's wedding. It was a perfect house for a reception and 200 people came. We all danced and it was a joyous event. On carnival days the house was full of people preparing for the procession and we always had a huge party there.

Now to end my story and to tell you what happened to Westport. My son and daughter-in law lived there for many years. They had three children, so they were able to enjoy it too. With some spare money they decided to make Westport a guest house, and I was delighted with all the improvements they made. The visitors all remarked on the happiness they felt while staying there.

Again sadness came, as my son and his family separated.

Soon I realised that Westport was too expensive for them to manage, so very reluctantly we decided to sell. I was hoping that another large family would be able to continue enjoying the happiness I had felt, but it was not to be, and after two years of waiting the only person able to buy Westport was a builder. You can imagine my horror when passing by one day I saw Westport being systematically knocked down. It was like a nightmare. Three ugly modern houses have been built in the garden. The people of Yarmouth shared my grief.

Now, every time I think of Westport I have mixed feelings of sadness and joy. that is why I wanted to write this obituary; to pay homage to a house that sheltered and loved me and my family for so many years.

*   *   *   *

Back to the timeline:

The next twenty years at Yarmouth went very smoothly. I was able to fulfil my urge to be a do-gooder! I started a Youth Club in the old railway station, and that is still going strong forty years on. There was an Approved School near us, run by Catholic Priests. Brother Cassian, the Headmaster, helped us with getting the Youth Club into working order, and we were all grateful. Imagine what horror the Island felt when headlines in the tabloids told us that he had been sacked for cruelty to the boys. It was all untrue so, armed with 8,000 signatures, I went off to the Home Office to protest. It was quite an ordeal waiting for hours to see the Home Secretary, with the Press hungry for interviews. Eventually Brother Cassian was exonerated, but the Approved School closed soon after that. I was glad that I'd had the courage to make a personal protest. I was also on the Steering Committee for the start of a Cheshire Home on the Island, and I became Chairman of the MIND campaign.

For light relief I was offered the job of being housekeeper to Bob Dylan when he came to sing at the Isle of Wight Pop Festival in 1969. This Pop Festival made the Island quite famous, and a quarter of a million young people invaded the Isle of Wight - most of us loved that. Bob Dylan wanted to bring his wife and children with him because they didn't want to use a hotel. The young organisers knew me well, so they hired a millionaire's house in Bembridge and gave me the job of cook-housekeeper and nanny. In the end Bob's children didn't come, but all the same I had a house party of ten to cook for and look after, so it was quite a task especially as Bob always wanted me to sit at the supper table with them and then he would sing to us. With my permission he invited George Harrison and his wife to join him at the house, so we were quite a family. I was really touched that George always helped me to clear away and wash up. He was an amusing person and very interested in the answers I gave to all his questions. It was a delight to listen to him and Bob singing together, and trying out new songs. Bob Dylan's band were staying at a nearby hotel, and they used to join in the fun in the evening. The Press used to surround the house, so I sent them off on shopping errands in return for any snippets of news about Bob. My children called in to meet Bob who was extremely courteous to them, but he had a job to get over his shyness.

On the day of the concert I was asked to prepare a buffet for about forty of Bob's famous friends. I refused because it meant missing the concert, so I was sacked. I appealed to Bob and he said he didn't want a party anyway so I was able to enjoy the concert from a VIP seat.

That was a pleasant but exhausting interlude in my life and I've 'milked' it ever since. It's nearly thirty years ago now, and I am often asked to recall my memories of that time on the local radio and by students researching the Isle of Wight Pop Festivals for their PhDs.

The silver wedding anniversary with my first husband was celebrated with great panache in the large garden of our house. About one hundred people came and we danced and chatted and had great fun. Sadly, my marriage break-up came soon after that occasion.

I became involved with three worthwhile charities in the 1970s, and they stood me in good stead when I was going through that depressing time. I met Leonard Cheshire when he came to the Island to persuade us to start a Cheshire Home. His delicate looks and shy charismatic charm completely floored me, and I found myself offering to start the first *friends group* and raise £1,000. This led to me being on the Steering Committee and being involved in finding a suitable Home for the disabled on the Island. We found a perfect place at Appley Cliff overlooking the sea at Shanklin, with a sheltered garden. Much had to be done to it but typically the Island people rallied and in no time at all the decorations had been done, and a lift installed. I met two nice young men in the pub where I was collecting. They belonged to Heals - the curtain and furniture shop - and they soon arranged for us to have all the material we needed for the large windows throughout the house. Two schools agreed to make the curtains.

And so, by 1973 the Home was ready to be opened by Leonard Cheshire. This year we are having a silver celebration for its 25th, and on Sunday July 26th 1998 all helpers and founder members were invited for a strawberry-and-cream tea.

My second charity work was for Hospital Radio, and I enjoyed this very much. To start with I helped with record requests, then a programme called *Happy Talk.* with Peter Baxter, but the most enjoyable and lasting programme was *Poetry Time* which I did first with my poet husband David Gascoyne, and later with Charles Loving. We kept this up for twenty-three years. Because of this I was given the job of interviewing Leonard Cheshire when he came to open the Home. This was an experience I shall never forget. He was a charming and easy interviewee and some of the advice he gave me has stayed in my heart.

The final charity work was one that virtually changed my life. I was asked to join the MIND Campaign on the Island and, before I knew it, I was made the chairman. This is a very worthwhile organisation because it helps the one in four of us who have mental breakdowns. I learnt all about it when I went to a National meeting at Church House, London, as the Island's delegate.

As part of my contribution to the MIND Campaign I used to go to the local Psychiatric Hospital once a week to read poetry to severely depressed patients. It used to touch me very much when they always came to my class and did their best to enjoy the poetry that I'd chosen to read to them. When I heard the shocking news that my husband had fallen in love with someone else, I felt so devastated that I didn't want to go on with my classes. However, either my conscience, or my religious beliefs, persuaded me that I should continue and that is why I went back to doing my once-a-week visit to the Hospital for poetry readings and discussions. One afternoon in February 1973, I chose to read a poem called *September Sun* from my Oxford Book of Verse. I told my class that it was a difficult poem written by a poet called David Gascoyne. When I had finished the reading, a tall sad-looking man touched me on the arm and said quietly, 'I wrote that poem, I am David Gascoyne'. I didn't really believe him until we were having a cup of tea together afterwards. He told me this was his third severe mental breakdown. 'What happens to you at weekends', I asked, because I knew that most of the wards closed down then. 'I go home to my empty house, and its very lonely', was the reply. I told him that I hated weekends too because my husband always went away with his lady friend. On an impulse I asked if he would come back to my house for the weekend if I came to fetch him. To my surprise he agreed. He seemed so terribly depressed and unhappy, that even talking was an effort for him.

Soon it became a habit and, in spite of myself, I found I was looking forward to the weekends when this sad looking giant would appear at the Hospital doors, clutching a carrier bag containing all his possessions.

We were able to enjoy certain things together, *Coronation Street* on the television and, on very special occasions, we used to go to a film together and stop off at a pub to discuss it on the way home. My teenage family were not too impressed by David, but they were tolerant enough because they thought he was making me less miserable. Back to the Hospital we used to go every Monday, and at one point my first husband Michael was at the same hospital having slowly recovered from a very forceful attempt at suicide.

Having both of them under psychiatric guidance was very wearisome. Eventually Michael came home, but things didn't go well. Finally I persuaded him to go away by himself for a week, and decide what he really wanted.

By a happy coincidence David had been sent £100 from the Royal Literary Fund, so we decided to go up to London together. This turned out to be an exciting week for us both. We stayed in separate rooms at the Basil Street Hotel in Knightsbridge, and David became very relaxed and confident. His old friend Antonia White called round to see him, and she and I became firm friends. Also, I met Alan Clodd of Enitharmon Press, who was David's publisher. He has been a faithful friend and David owes a great deal to him. Alan took us to the British Library which was holding an exhibition of *Poets in the Thirties.* Much of David's work was on display, with handsome photographs of him when he was young. When we weren't meeting David's friends we went off to art galleries. This was quite an experience for me because David is a real expert on art. We also went to plays and a musical called *Flowers,* by Lindsay Kemp. The days went by far too quickly. I would like to recall one silly little anecdote which shows me up in all my naiveté - David's watch had broken and he was lost without it because he had an obsession with time at that point. I told him not to worry because I'd seen some good watches in the window of an arcade near our hotel. They were priced at £4.50 and £7.50, or so I thought. While sitting on the golden chairs with a very obsequious shopkeeper, I realised to my alarm that the watches were actually £450 and £750. When I told the man from Aspreys that I thought it was an absurd price for a watch, he told us quite rudely that we could get what we wanted at a supermarket. 'And indeed we will', I told him.

The climax of our week in London happened at the Poetry Society in Earl's Court. I had secretly arranged that David might give a reading there on our last night. We went along expecting to see two or three of David's old friends, but when we entered the room it was packed out, and everyone gave him a great welcome. He read from his collected poems in a clear and assured voice, and I was astounded. This brought about an invitation to the 1st International Poetry Festival at Cambridge, which was to take place the next year.

While we were walking to the Poetry Centre, I noticed a tall man walking beside me. 'Are you a poet?', I asked him. 'I leave that for others to judge', he said. David turned to me and said, 'That is John Heath-Stubbs, and he's just won the Queen's medal for poetry'. I felt so happy to be mixing in a world of poets.

All good things come to an end and back we had to go to the Isle of Wight. Michael had returned from his holiday and told me that he couldn't live without his new love. Almost without realising it I said, 'That's fine because I have fallen in love with David Gascoyne'.

I waited until I took David his breakfast in bed at 8.30 am the next morning, and told him everything. He listened intently and then said, *Well, I'll be a most frustrating husband, but if you are brave enough to risk it, so am I!* So that was the start of a new life for us both.

Quite a few things had to be sorted out in David's house before we could move there together, but it didn't take long, and we settled in one chilly evening on September 23rd 1974. The days went by quickly and quietly. David spent most of the time in his room, and I set about turning the house into a home. I made quite a few mistakes with my cooking, not realising that David was diabetic. I used to give him iced cakes for tea, and plenty of delicious desserts. The doctor called and put a stop to all that. I had not realised that diabetes is something you don't recover from. David has to take the full quota of pills now, but he keeps quite well and we have a monthly visit from a diabetic expert.

The divorce became absolute in April, and we arranged to be married on May 17th 1975. Before it took place we had a visit from an official solicitor who had been in charge of all David's affairs during his mental breakdown. He sent me out of the room and asked David if he really did want to marry me! After nearly twenty-four years I wonder if he remembers that visit? I have always enjoyed keeping diaries, and I've kept one ever since I met David. It is extremely useful for checking dates and people's names. Another thing that gave me great pleasure was discovering that David's wild garden was really beautiful, with a pond and lawns and very overgrown flower beds. There is something very soothing, but very time-consuming, in discovering a secret garden. Its still my favourite place, even though I have to rely on others to help me with it now. I'm writing this on a hot July evening in 1998. Northwood is a very small and friendly village, and the church gives me much pleasure and comfort.

I suppose the first big event that we were asked to was the Cambridge International Poetry Festival. This took place just before our marriage. Poor David was knocked down by a Cambridge bike, and he broke his collarbone, but that didn't stop him giving a very good reading, and also a television interview. I was starting to think that I'd married someone very famous, and very stoic!

The next excitement was an invitation to a Royal Garden Party. David is on the Queen's Civil List, and he'd been asked before and refused. This time I made him accept and we had a really enjoyable time there. Harold Wilson and his poet wife, Mary, joined our table for tea. While David flattered Mary about her poetry I showed off about my famous relation, Stafford Cripps, and Harold Wilson said he admired him very much. The day went well from start to finish.

Hot on the heels of this we attended a symposium of the *Poets of the Thirties* at the University of East Anglia. We stayed at the home of George Barker and went every day to lavish receptions and readings. Anthony Thwaite was a most cordial organiser, and we had a joyful barbecue with Stephen Spender who was in great form. All this happened during the heatwave summer of 1976.

When Alan Clodd came to stay with us in Northwood, we rediscovered David's journals. They had been written in Paris when he was very young. I loved reading them because it was like meeting David as a young man.

Alan decided to publish them and they went down very well. Years later they were translated into French by Christine Jordis in Paris, and we had a week of media attention over that.

But I digress as always, it is so hard to condense a lifetime into a short book. I find it difficult to make up my mind what to write and what to leave out.

I think I should make another mention of our marriage. This took place at Newport Town Hall and David's friend, Neville Braybrooke, was our best man and his wife, June, my matron of honour. She brought such a sense of fun into our lives, and since her death we miss her dreadfully. Neville made a really good speech at the reception held in our tiny house. About forty of us were there, and I made very simple sandwiches and a wedding cake. We left for the ceremony with David's nephew Edward and all my family came with their children. We received lots of telegrams which they don't send nowadays. Every anniversary I bring out all these souvenirs. We didn't have a honeymoon, but we went to dinner at the Farringford Hotel which was Tennyson's old house.

Then we went back to normal; every Sunday night David came to read with me for Hospital Radio. I suppose the next big event in out lives was the invitation to read at the British Consulate in Paris. Again, David knew that I would be really disappointed if he refused, so off we went in the Spring of 1979.

Again, that was an amazing experience for me. To begin with I was feeling a bit ill with 'flu and I had to spend the first day in the hotel bedroom whilst David explored the pharmacies for me. Thankfully I was well enough to go to David's reading the next day. It was followed by a banquet given by the Embassy. The food and the company were unforgettable. On this first visit we met Christine Jordis and her family. She was as nice as she was beautiful, and after a few years she set about translating David's journals into French. We have remained great friends for over twenty years, and Le Monde sent her over to stay with us in 1997 after David had won a Chevalier award. After a week in Paris we came back to the Isle of Wight and settled down for a while. We used to visit Paris at least three times a year, mostly for David to talk to students at the Sorbonne. Once he talked about the *Art of Translation* at a big conference held at the British Institute which was very good. On one special visit we met Simon Callow with the Royal Shakespeare Company who were visiting Paris. He read some of David's poems at an evening of poetry and music at the British Institute. We have remained friends with Simon ever since, and he has been so generous and helpful to David. He has also taken part in a broadcast of one of David's play *Procession to the Private Sector* on Radio 3 recently..

A little bit of family life came back when we were not touring the world. My daughter Sue has three children, so on some special weekends I thought it would be nice if they all came to stay with us. It gave me a chance to do a spot of mothering, and they were all so good. They slept together in one huge bed in the spare room. Jake 2, Warren 4 and Emma in charge, aged 8. They had to follow my old-fashioned routine of going to bed at 6 pm, or at least preparing for it with a long bath, supper and stories! By 7 pm they were not only settled but usually asleep. I enjoy recalling those days with them. We used to go blackberrying and, during the month of May, we used to picnic in the bluebell woods nearby. I don't think I have been a very useful grandmother, but I do cherish those memories. Jake, who is now in his twenties and travelling the world doing drama plays, used to climb up on David's lap when he was about two, and fall asleep for an hour or two. David didn't mind because ever since I've known him he has always been able to sit without fidgeting for hours at a time. Now its only Thomas our cat who likes to curl up with him.

While David was too depressed to read much to himself, something rather nice happened. He asked me if I would like to read the First Volume of Proust to him bit by bit. This became a most pleasant ritual. Every day between 2 and 2.30, I read from *Swann's Way*. I've never had the discipline to read the well-known classics since I was about sixteen, but the reading of Proust to David was a revelation. I enjoyed it so much and during three months we finished all the volumes.

When the grandchildren came to stay they all knew that they must disappear or remain silent until the ritual reading was over. We continued later with Dickens and other classics, but nothing equalled the joy I had in reading Proust.

Soon after our frequent visits to Paris, David started translating again. This has always been his forte, and it helped bridge the gap between writing his own poetry. I decided to improve my French by giving lessons. It only needed a notice in the Parish magazine and one in the window for me to have enough students at every stage of the language to keep me happy. I also taught elocution, English and reading. After eighteen years I have as many pupils as I need and it keeps me in pocket money and in touch with the young. I suppose the saying, 'Once a teacher, always a teacher' is a true one. I learned the art of giving talks at the WI College called Denman, where I stayed for five days. Miss Bird, who was a prestigious teacher at Princess Anne's school - Beneden, taught us all very well, and we promised her we would always agree to give talks when asked. After over thirty years I realise what an amazing teacher she was. I give about twelve talks a year and, recalling her strict teaching, I can honestly say I make quite a good job of it.

Now that we are both so crippled, I relive all the amazing world poetry festivals and visits abroad by giving talks to the WIs or TWGs, called *Travels with a Poet*. I've also taken my camera with me everywhere which means I can visually re-live all our travels.

Before I met David I had never been in an aeroplane or travelled abroad. It was good to be at the 1st World Festival of Poetry at Ostia near Rome. This much resembled the Pop Festival on the Isle of Wight. It took place on the beach every night with literally hundreds of excited young poetry fans. The Americans played a large part in it. When the 'Beach Boys', as we called them, grew tired of the endless recitals of poetry in every language, they started to hurl rocks onto the huge stage, shouting 'Basta, Basta'. This apparently means 'enough, enough'. I vividly recall Allen Ginsberg and Peter Orlovski helping David and myself down a ladder from the stage. Then Allen restored order by reciting and singing with his guitar. The press and television people were vastly excited about this. On the last night the whole stage collapsed, but no-one was badly hurt.

A strange part of that Festival was that we were all put up in a disused hotel. We had bedrooms, but there was no food so David and I had to go in search of breakfast on the beach. At other times we used to eat in the restaurant of the Piscine. In the evenings at the concert there were endless little stalls on the beach, which sold all kinds of food. George Barker and David found much to amuse them at that Festival. Also, through going there, Lawrence Ferlinghetti invited David to read at *The City Lights* in San Francisco, and Allen Ginsberg arranged for him to do readings all over New York. Both these events would really take a chapter each, but I will try to relive them on a page or two. I felt a bit nervous about our departure from Heathrow to New York, because it was a long flight. Also, we were going to be away for six weeks, which is the longest 'gig' we have ever had. One of the trials I've had to cope with all my life is the awful homesickness I suffer when away. But this was an exciting trip and I soon forgot about our house in the Isle of Wight.

The departure from Heathrow was memorable. Kevin and Sheena had driven us up at the crack of dawn. One of the penalties of living on this Island is that all travelling takes about two hours longer.

When we arrived at Heathrow my son Milo and his family were there, and also my daughter Jenny. The anxiety was much soothed by the drinking of a bottle of whisky. The flight was longer than I expected, but we watched a colour film and then the clocks went back for five hours, so we arrived soon after we'd started, if you follow me. I was not impressed with the treatment by the passport authorities; a gimlet-eyed lady gave David quite a hard time. He was patient up to a point, and then demanded for us to go through. A Yellow Cab was called and in the excitement of it all, we didn't notice that we had left David's overnight bag at the airport, full of precious diabetic pills and money. We had a smart address, Fifth Avenue, and our apartment was very elegant. It was the place where visiting professors stay when they come to lecture at the NU. I well remember how thrilled I was looking out of the windows at a typical New York night scene full of sky-scrapers all lit up. We both decided to take a nap before venturing forth for our evening meal. To our horror David's overnight bag was nowhere to be found, and calls to the Yellow Cab centre and Kennedy Airport drew a blank.

We were due to dine with David's artist friend, Buffi Johnson. She had prepared a wonderful meal. We were able to ring Mrs Balakian, our hostess, who in no time had contacted a psychoanalyst from our block of flats, who was ready and willing to provide us with prescriptions and money. All she seemed to want was a copy of David's *Collected Poems,* so that particular crisis was averted. Months later when we had returned to the Isle of Wight the overnight case was returned to us free of charge and with nothing missing.

We made good use of the apartment which had a kitchen with stores already provided. We had lots of 'phone calls before going out. Allen Ginsberg came to welcome us and tell us of all the bookings he had made. We gave a party at the flat, and it went with a swing.

*   *   *   *

I must say a few words here about the Beat Poets, and especially Allen Ginsberg, sadly no longer with us.

Gregory Corso was telling Lawrence Ferlinghetti that he had offered David some dope, but although David had not been interested, his 'Old Lady' had said 'No Way'. David overheard and we laughed about it often.

My overall impression of the Beats was that they were not very polite, and one called me a stuck-up prig. However, Allen Ginsberg and Lawrence Ferlinghetti were quite different. They were easy to talk to, very kind and considerate. They both took great care of us during the near-riot at the Ostia Poetry festival. Their planning and support made the six weeks in the US possible, they arranged events and paid for many things for us. Both Allen and Lawrence enjoyed talking with David, who teased them a bit.

On other occasions I met them, I noted how generous and kind they were, and how unconceited. When Allen and David appeared at NU to answer questions on surrealism, the event was reported in the New York Times under the heading The Surrealist and the Bumpkin, Allen had willingly classed himself as the Bumpkin!

*　　　*　　　*　　　*

David's first major event was giving a talk at the NU about surrealism. It was very well attended and written about in the press. David's friends, the Shaw-Lawrences were there; he'd known them when he was only seventeen at Teddington. After three days of complete luxury on Fifth Avenue, we booked rooms at the Chelsea Hotel with Mr Bard in charge. This is a famous old hotel, and Mr Bard is very snobby about all the famous poets and writers who have stayed with him. Dylan Thomas actually died there, having over-indulged in alcohol while on a reading tour in 1953. New York hotels are different from ours, they provide kitchens and its rather like hiring a bed-sitter. It was scruffy but useful. The 'phone rings all day in New York because I believe local calls are free. There we remained for a rip-roaring week. The American hospitality is legendary, and we were not disappointed. In between David's readings we were given receptions with enormous quantities of food and drink. A memorable supper was with Erika Duncan and Buffi Johnson in Greenwich Village, where Erika lives with her three children. Erika had been to our home to write a chapter about David, which she had entitled *My weekend with a Silent Poet.* We had a good time with her, but I found myself dropping off to sleep over dinner. Something I hadn't expected about New York was the lively atmosphere, and during the day I felt I could do anything! This was just as well because Allen Ginsberg had organised many readings. However, David managed to take me to the Museum of Modern Art which was absorbing but exhausting. When we returned to the Chelsea we both fell asleep for two hours. Luckily Laurence Weisburt rang to remind us that we were due for a reading with Tom Pickard. So off we went to that, in an elegant black and white studio where the audience all sat on cushions on the floor.

Another thing we did on our own was to visit the Cloisters about two miles out of New York. It was looking beautiful in the snow. We also took tea at the Chelsea with Virgil Thomson, the composer. He was witty and courteous and made us mushroom sandwiches. The rest of the time was taken up with lavish receptions. The story of how David and I met seemed to intrigue the romantic

Americans no end. After ten very busy days we were ready to fly off to San Francisco.

David's sister-in-law, Joan Gascoyne, met us at San Francisco Airport and drove us to her apartment. Joan is such a generous loving person; her husband, David's brother, died most sadly of cancer when only in his fifties, and she has been so brave about it. I wish I could have know him. His twin brother also died of cancer, much too young. Anyway, Joan made us most welcome and she had given up her bedroom for us.

The three weeks in San Francisco passed very swiftly. We visited Alcatraz island by boat. David spent an afternoon with Thom Gunn in the Japanese Garden. Friends of Joan's and the Fixels came to call. The climax was David's reading at *The City Lights,* which was beautifully organised by Nancy and Laurence. The place was packed out with American poets and other celebrities. We all drank wine and ate strawberries, and David and I were in our element.

Towards the end of our stay Joan had a nasty bout of the 'flu, and I'm sure she longed to be in her own bedroom again. We rang up Larry Fixel and his wife, and he said, 'Come on over and stay with us, we have an empty flat'. So we packed our bags and when we arrived he opened the door and said, 'Have you heard the news?' We hadn't, so he told us that Ronald Reagan had been shot at, but was recovering in hospital. The media had a field day, and all the TV programmes carried news of the attempted assassination all day. Eventually we were told that Reagan would recover, but it was a memorable day.

We enjoyed being with the Fixels. He is a writer of some repute, and Justine is a psychologist and totally charming. We have kept in touch but they are both ageing now and not very well.

They took us to Santa Cruz for a memorable day with an old friend of David's, George Woodcock, who was having an all-day party. On the way home by the Pacific Coast Highway, I paddled in the Pacific; the coastline reminded me a little of the Isle of Wight.

I dashed around the shops of San Francisco for souvenirs for the family. I didn't obey Larry Fixel's advice *Admire but don't acquire.* We rang Joan to say goodbye. She was feeling much better and took us to the airport to catch the plane. We flew away on a beautiful evening. During the night we flew over the North Pole and the stewardess let me have a good look while the others were all dozing. It was stunningly beautiful.

Back to Heathrow again and eventually to the Isle of Wight. While we were away some of my family had completely refitted the kitchen as a surprise. Mary, my surrogate daughter from Yarmouth, had put a shelf up in David's bedroom so that he had somewhere to write. That soon started him off, and many a new poem and good obituary has been written on that bedroom shelf. Mary has been a very close friend all through my life on the Island.

We both had a touch of jet-lag upon our return, which was a nuisance because there was so much to do.

We were warmly welcomed back to Hospital Radio and my church gave me a special welcome too. Then we had a Paris trip to organize for May 1981. This was quite a special visit. The Sorbonne professors had decided to give a *Homage to David Gascoyne* at the Pompidou Centre. So many arrangements had to be made. David sat on the platform while very fulsome tributes were made to him. Also readings from his Paris Journal by John Edwards, and extracts from his poems were read by Vivienne Forrester.

It was an exciting experience for me and my daughter, Sue, who came with us for our week in Paris. It coincided with the election of President Mitterand, so Sue and I had a good time in the streets near our hotel. We cheered with all the other Parisians when he paid a visit to Pontheon. Its funny because I've always hated the thought of going to big occasions in the crowds in London, but in Paris it was quite different. Quite a few of David's writer friends were in the crowds so we had a good time. David had a date with old friends and we dined with them later.

Probably because of our visit to America with all the delicious receptions, I discovered to my dismay that I had put on two stones in weight and I was approaching the dreaded thirteen stones. So off I went, with much misgivings, to an afternoon Weight Watchers class in Newport. In some ways it was better than I expected, but in others it was more disciplined. We were weighed, then we had a pep talk, and then we were given a diet sheet for the week. It entailed weighing all that we ate, and cutting out alcohol. That was the worst part! Although it took ages, over a year in fact, I did gain my goal weight which I thought was an impossible joke. I was given a gold badge and card. Like everyone else I swore I would never put the weight back on, but like everyone else I did. I took about fifteen years to do it. I blame my arthritis, coupled with laziness and greediness. Nevertheless I'm proud that I did lose so much weight and often brazenly say that I could do it again.

The other thing I wanted to write about before continuing with my 'travelogue', was the time I spent teaching at Westmont School in Newport. By another coincidence, the headmistress of a small private school rang to ask if I would like to do some part-time teaching there. The idea pleased me and most afternoons I went to teach elocution and poetry. It entailed teaching all the different classes and I enjoyed it very much. An added pleasure was that my two grandsons were at the school. Also I had an extra challenge, the headmistress, Jan Maclean, asked if I would put in as many pupils as possible for the verse-speaking competition held every year at Ryde Festival. The children did well and it gave the school a good name. I was able to do this for two or three years before David's commitments abroad became too intrusive. In the past I had often entered Ryde Festival for verse-speaking and drama, and I enjoyed it very much. My son Milo and I entered a Shakespeare duologue from Macbeth when he was only seven, and we both enjoyed that. When I found that reciting long poems from memory was too much of a task, I asked the organisers if we could have a class for poetry reading. This attracted many more entries, but I didn't often win the cup that I donated.

Drama has also had a warm spot in my life. Soon after arriving on the Island I joined the West Wight Drama Group. My first big part was in *The Inspector Calls*. I loved the rehearsals and the performances. Golly Mitchell, an ex-Japanese prisoner-of-war was the Inspector, and Nell Goodwin was the Director. J B Priestley was living on the Island at the time, and he sent us a good luck card. Several other good parts came my way - *A Phoenix too Frequent* by Christopher Fry was very well directed by Elizabeth Bowyer, and we performed it all over the Island, most notably at Carisbrooke Castle.

An interesting experience came my way when I was asked to act with some prisoners at Albany Jail on the Isle of Wight. John Carver, the producer, suggested that we put on *The Black Sheep of the Family,* a Whitehall farce. The prisoners loved it and all the officers came to the performance. I had to make a speech at the end, and referred to the officers as 'screws', much to the inmates amusement. It made for a good atmosphere and I was sorry when it was decided that outside amateur theatrical groups would not be allowed to take part any more.

All these events took place in the sixties. During that time my poor mother died in a Nursing Home. Her Alzheimer's had become very difficult, and my father couldn't manage to look after her on his own. However, we did have a very beautiful memorial service for my mother at Marlow. She had been much loved and her hospitality and her love of helping everyone were legendary.

My father died seven years later. He had been surviving on his own at his home in Marlow, called *Redpits,* where Sue had been born. He died, as he had often planned with me, in his lovely garden. When Michael held me in his arms and told me of Guy's death, I felt very lost and made preparations to get to Marlow for his funeral. My father, Guy, was much loved by everyone. When I told my best friend Marion that he had died, she burst into tears in the shop, and she had only met him once. Guy had a Catholic funeral, although marrying my mother had kept him from his faith because she was a Protestant. During the 1st World War when he was so badly wounded in the head, he had received extreme unction from the Pope because he was expected to die. Severely disabled, he also suffered from severe migraines because of it for the rest of his life. He was a very brave man and never complained about his disabilities.

Guy's funeral at the Catholic Church in Marlow was full of young people. He had an affinity with the young and now, nearly forty years on, I'm often told how much he had helped them and how they had wanted to be like him. My brothers and I were very sad but we were proud too. I love it when I see them both, and we can talk about our parents.

While I write these memories I am puzzled by what to record and what to leave out. I have always been fascinated by the computer-like brain we've been given which records our lives. I believe you should feed it with positive thoughts, then it will let you achieve anything. Nevertheless, my computer brain remembers things in a bit of a jumble. I want to write about 1984 now, regardless of where I was before.

Early Years

1984

It was quite a watershed for both David and me. Having kept a diary every day, its quite tempting to record every year as it comes, but instead I think I'll just record special events as they come to mind. In 1984 David wrote a monologue for Radio called *Self-Discharged.* It was about the time he spent at an asylum in Epsom. It is written with humour and pathos, and the radio programme was a success. We have it on tape and I enjoy listening to it. Early in that year we flew to Paris in a tiny plane, in a gale, which was hairy. It was for the launching of David's Journals in French, translated by Christine Jordis. We had plenty of media attention, including a television news crew at our hotel. They asked David dozens of questions, which he answered in fluent French. What amused me was the fact that the Patron of the hotel felt that TV programme was using up too much electricity; in spite of the fact that David was telling the Paris listeners why we always used this hotel. Apparently, Luis Buñuel the film maker always used it too. We didn't know this until years later.

Every single newspaper in Paris offered us hospitality in return for full-page interviews with photographs. So entirely different from the attitude of the English papers on the subject of poets and book publishing! I've kept all the cuttings and they make pleasant reading.

On our return to England we went off to Ted Hughes' organization at Totleigh Barton. This takes place at an old picturesque cottage in Devon. Aspiring poets and writers get help from a poet in residence, and this time it was John Fairfax. At the weekend they invite a special poet to read their works. A beautiful meal is prepared and served by the students themselves. David has been invited three times, and its always been very special. It was a brilliant idea of Ted Hughes' and its been going for years now.

Also in that year the *Adam International Review* celebrated fifty years under the editorship of Miron Grindea, and there was a memorable concert at the French Institute with all Miron's favourites taking part. I recall John Ogden's piano playing and Christopher Fry giving an excellent talk.

Sadly in that year our friend [Meary James Thurairajah] Tambi[muttu], editor of *Poetry London* and publisher in 1943 of David's *Poems 1937-1942,* died, and there was a memorial concert for him. We went to London on July 13th to help with the five-hundredth celebrations of St James, Piccadilly. I recall the Reverend Donald Reeves asking us all to sing Happy Birthday to the Church. The Queen Mother attended, and after the service there was a lavish spread in a marquee with plenty of champagne. David and I were presented to the Queen Mother, and she was every bit as lovely and easy to talk to as I had expected.

Also in 1984 we flew off to Dublin for an Irish Tour for *Poetry Ireland,* arranged by Michael Longley. This was good too. We stayed in Dublin to begin with, and David was on a radio chat show with a Terry Wogan type of man. As a result, his reading at Basalis, the famous old Hotel, was a complete sell-out. The Irish have a great respect for Poets, and the right attitude to life. David also read at the Universities in Belfast, Athlone and Galway, where we met up with old friends. We then gave a reading for John Montague in Cork. Finally, we returned to Dublin for a great final reading, and we were seen off in style at Dublin Airport. It's a very heart-warming experience to be in Ireland among so many appreciative poets, but the news as I write (1998) after the Omagh bombing fills my heart with dread.

I must continue with 1984. I used to think Orwell was mad to write about a year so far ahead. Now its over and gone, and I must adjust myself to the thought that I may, after all, be alive in the year 2000. The year 1984 brought an invitation from Louvain for a World Poetry Festival. David was the President for that, and he made a good speech at the closing reception. Guillevic, an elderly Breton poet, was there. He and David held a discussion together on the stage on the subject of the Poet and the Town. David was asked about his long radio poem called *Night Thoughts* which was about London.

When the Festival as over, we were invited by the Lebanese Ambassador, Salah Stétié, to stay in his house in The Hague in Holland. This was quite an experience for me because it was strange to be in an Embassy House and to be waited on hand and foot. I was also intrigued by the different political discussions that went on. A dear old lady who had been a famous hostess in Paris was staying with us, and I enjoyed listening to her recollections about Paris in the thirties.

At last it was time to return home, where the mounds of mail were always a bit daunting after being away. We were preparing in the Autumn for our tour of the French Universities, due to the fact that David had been chosen for the Agrégation. This meant that all higher grade students would be studying his work.

So off we went to Paris in the late autumn. Firstly, a big poetry reading and Homage to David, by the Sorbonne Professors. They had huge blown-up photographs of David in the Bookshop window. When we arrived the room was full, and then we had to listen to Michel Rely, John Roberts and Francois Xavier, paying their tributes to David before he actually started reading. I always enjoy hearing French spoken, even if I can't quite understand it. After the reading the champagne flowed and the food was delicious. The French really know how to give receptions.

The next day we were off to Bordeaux. The University had sent Michele Duclos to escort us down there. When we arrived at the crowded Garde de LasT, David said he wanted to get a paper so off he went, and Michele and I waited at the Quai, where the train for Bordeaux was nearly due to depart. After half and hour there was no sign of David, and we worked ourselves into an absurd panic. We asked for a notice to be given out telling Mr David Gascoyne to meet us at the train platform. Still there was no sign of him, and we even believed that he'd been kidnapped! We were sure David couldn't have caught the train because he had no ticket, and the French are rather severe about this. After some hours of panic we had a call from the Bordeaux University to say that David had been met by Régis Rex, and was safe and well. Michele and I caught the next train and celebrated with a little whisky with our meal.

By the time we eventually arrived, David was settling down to a delicious dinner prepared for him by the catering students at the University. He was amused by our concern and then there was much laughter and rejoicing.

The next day David spoke to the students and read some poetry, and I was asked to give a fairly amusing account of David's disappearing act at the Gare de LAST.

There were no lectures and we were soon back in Paris being chauffeur driven in a British Consul car to the Gare de LAST on our way to Nancy where Michel Rely was awaiting us most eagerly. Nancy is a very glitzy town, and we enjoyed our stay there very much. Michel worked David very hard, and the food was delicious. After three days there, Michel drove us the 300 miles back to Paris. He is a fast driver and excellent company, as was his beautiful Persian girlfriend, Susie. We landed up with some Irish poets at Shakespeare & Company. George Whitman makes a tremendous fuss of his visiting poets, but he isn't as polite and gracious to his staff.

After a few days of recovery in Paris, we were off to the T.V. on a very fast train to Lyons, for the last lap of our tour.

Adolphe Haberer met us off the train, gave us lunch and then it was University time again. After the talk and reception, we were driven to Lozanne, a small village near Lyons, where we stayed for two nights. The next day we were taken on a very interesting tour of Lyons with Adolphe's children.

The evening was spent at a party at the house where we stayed, which was charmingly organised. About fifty people came and, at the end of the party, David was persuaded to read some of his poetry.

The next day we were put on the lunchtime train for Paris. I didn't mind leaving too much, because I knew we had a date to dine with Larry Durrell at La Coupole. I was anxious to meet him because he had been very kind to

David in the early days in Paris, and that they had a mutual respect for each other.

So back to Hotel St Pierre to unpack and get 'poshed up' for Larry's dinner party. I wasn't expecting to come under his charm so easily, especially as he was then drinking only Perrier water, but Larry is Larry, drunk or sober and we had the most hilarious evening. Larry's friend was with him, but it seemed that all the guests at La Coupole were joining in the general joie de vivre that Larry Durrell gives to us all.

By the time we returned to England, it was time to make plans for Christmas, which I always take quite seriously. I agonise over what to give to whom, and I try to realise that the grandchildren are getting quite grown-up and would probably prefer money! Nevertheless, I prepare a box of unsuitable presents all through the year, and then wrap them in pretty paper and hope for the best. My elder daughter, Sue, and her charming dentist husband, Miles, nearly always take on the mammoth task of having eighteen of us for Christmas Lunch. Sue has the most amazing capacity for calm, and it's all done as if it were no trouble at all, but I know that behind the scenes she works really hard and plans with great care. Every year I inflict an extra elderly person on her. David says I am a 'gerontophile' and, in a way, I suppose I am, but I get great pleasure and friendship from my elderly friends. I note in my 1984 diary that it was old Will Russell's turn. He was a funny old character. I befriended him and his wife when our vicar let it be known that they would like to be taken shopping occasionally, but it turned out to be quite a commitment. His wife was severely crippled at the end of their marriage, and he didn't cope very well. Will had been gassed in the First World War, and he felt that he should be waited on for ever after. But he often made me laugh with his silly cockney jokes. He was quite a nuisance at the Christmas Lunch, but the family found him highly amusing. He lived to be ninety-two and expected me to organise good birthday parties for him in the local pub.

Anyway, Christmas was as usual that year with Kevin, my elder son and a complete extrovert, giving out the presents. As the family opened them with cries of glee, it made me feel that at that stage of Christmas they would have been pleased with anything. 'Christmas is the best of times, and the worst of times', to misquote Dickens in his *Tale of Two Cities*.

I recall our farm Christmases where it always seemed to be cold and snowy. My brothers and I had lavish presents from rich friends who Ben used to call 'Our patrons'. My Godmother used to send me superb dolls with their clothes and equipment from Harrods, and the boys had Meccano sets and small steam engines. My father always filled me a stocking, but I can't remember believing in Father Christmas! My mother thought it unnecessary for us to have a Christmas tree, because we used to go to so many parties where we could see other people's trees. Secretly I yearned for one of our own, so ever since I left home for marriage a Christmas tree has been the most important part of my preparations. When the children were small, Michael and I did our best to fill old long knitted stockings with suitable things. I recall Milo running into our room with his stocking saying, 'He's comed!'

Years later when the children were teenagers, they filled two stockings for us, full of hilarious things! The best Christmases were when the children were small, and when Michael didn't have any veterinary calls. Kevin went into the hotel trade, and Sue became a nurse, so they were always working over Christmas and I found it hard to make much of it when that happened. After my second marriage it was enjoyable to go to Sue's for the big day with all the grandchildren. One year I thought it would be marvellous to hire the Church Hall, and have them all as our guests for a change. But it turned out to be quite difficult because I had to put the turkey in the oven in the kitchen in the cold dark hall on my way back from the midnight service. Although the family all rallied to help me, I found coping for twenty-four almost more than I could manage. It wasn't David's 'scene' to help out much!

However, we did have fun in the Church Hall. Sue had brought over a stranded German sailor, who helped with the festivities. The grandchildren with their other grandmother put on an amusing sing-song on the stage. The worst part was washing it all up at about 6 pm and leaving the hall tidy. I'm afraid we didn't repeat the experience.

Christmas now is rather low key because its too much of a hassle to get David over to Yarmouth in his wheelchair, especially as I'm crippled too. But we enjoy the peace of the day on our own. Before that there are endless good visits from all the family, and the church services play a big part in my Christmas enjoyment. It always amuses me how every year I pretend that I don't like Christmas at all, and yet every year I enjoy it more than ever.

1985

Now back to the eighties which have been such a good decade to look back on. Out of the blue David heard from an Italian poet friend that he had won the *1982 Biella prize for a foreign poet.* This was very special and a great surprise. We flew off to Milan and went to Roberto Sanesi's house; then after tea he drove us the seventy miles to Biella, a charming old Mediaeval town, where the ceremony was to take place the next day. We went to our hotel and I changed into a long white cotton dress, which I rather fancied myself in. At the Banquet I was told I looked like Lady Macbeth! I wasn't sure if that was a compliment or not! As always, the Italian meal was marvellous. I had just reached my goal weight for Weight Watchers, so I threw caution to the winds!

The next day was the big prize giving in the Town Hall. The stage was decorated with flowers and girls in National Costume. The jury for the award were on the stage and the Minister of Culture and members of the British Council. David and Roberto were on the platform too. The Minister of Culture made a fulsome speech and presented David with a heavy silver plaque suitably engraved. Later, David was asked to read his poem called *Mountains* and he was presented with two large books with paintings of Mountains. By 1 pm the ceremony was over, and we all went to the Town Hall for a really lavish banquet. The Italians really know how to spoil you.

Later Roberto drove us back to Milan where we were booked in at a most elegant hotel in a quiet square for two or three nights. We enjoyed Milan very much, but decided to spend some of the four million Lire which was part of the prize on a few days in Venice, a place I'd never thought to visit except in my dreams. It came up to my expectations. We stayed in a quiet part of Venice, and for one whole week we had a very special time. I loved going on the Vaporetti. We visited the graves of Stravinski, Diaghilev and Ezra Pound. We had a day at the Lido where David hired a deck-chair and looked like Dirk Bogarde in the film *Death in Venice.* I swam happily in the Adriatic. We had a delicious picnic lunch and then went on to visit Peter Russell, a poet friend of David's. He lived in a cottage with his wife and two small children,. and he was pleased to meet up with David again. Out visit to Venice went too quickly. We were able to indulge ourselves because we had to spend most of the four million Lire before our return to England. This wasn't very difficult because we had gorgeous meals, went on a gondola, and visited museums. Two highlights were a visit to Peggy Guggenheim's museum. David recalled visiting her when he stayed in Venice in the fifties. Also, the Venice *Biennale* was on and we visited that, meeting a young sculptor who had won a prestigious prize for his sculpture of *Hares.*

So back to Milan for three more good days at the Hotel Manzoni. Recalling these days of excitement and luxury, they take on the feeling that I must have dreamt it all. Back to a bit of family life and mounds of letters to answer. In those days David cheerfully took it all on, although it took up a lot of time and kept him from writing. During that year I met David's friend Roland Penrose, and his partner Diane Diareze. He invited us to Paris for his *Vernissage* which was an elegant affair. Roland is the most charming of men, and a faithful friend. We had some good weekends at his house in Chiddingly in West Sussex. Another trip to Paris before that year was up came as a pleasant surprise. David invited me to read some of his poetry with him at the Sorbonne.

An invitation out of the blue came from Lambeth Palace. Robert Runcie wanted to promote more poetry to be read in Churches and Cathedrals. So he collected six poets and the Bishop of Oxford to host a lunch with that in mind. I drove David up to the Palace and we stayed in one of the guest rooms. I quickly realised that I wasn't on the luncheon guest list, and I was wondering where to put myself! However, I really had the best of it because I was invited to have lunch with Terry Waite in the kitchen. This was something I shall never forget. He made me a 'cup-a-soup' and we had bread and cheese. He's the sort of person that makes you want to do better, but for all his kindness he has a great sense of humour, so we laughed all the time. As he left, I knew that he was off on a mission to try to free some hostages in Beirut. When his own capture came, I was devastated and found it difficult to relax. The day of his release was a really marvellous day for us all.

One thing he said that amused me was 'It's a question of Poets and Peasants, poets upstairs and peasants downstairs'. When he left I went upstairs and was invited to join in the discussion, with tea and cakes. Nothing much came of it, but for us it was quite a turning point.

We stayed in the Palace guest house with Bishop Hook and his wife Ruth. Both were totally charming, and very 'in' to poetry. They invited Julian and Anthony Harvey from Westminster Abbey to join us for supper, and we all became firm friends. What was rather special was the fact that Canon Harvey and his wife always invited us to stay with them at the Abbey when we were in London. It was a perfect resting place with no parking problems! Also there were some interesting Abbey occasions to attend. These events lead me to believe that one good thing nearly always leads me to another.

I suppose the next big step was a visit to Iceland during a windy September in 1985. I had rather stupid ideas about what it would be like. We had to drive to Heathrow again because of a train strike. The flight to Iceland was via Glasgow, which was a bit tedious, and we arrived about twenty miles from Reykjavik. We were met by a young friend from Paris, David Appleyard, who drove us to our Saga Hotel. As expected, the countryside made me feel that I was actually on the moon, especially as there were very few houses. The hotel was good. The reception was at a newly built hall, and we were warmly received by Thor Williamson and all the other poets. They were mostly from the Nordic lands, but Canada was represented and, best of all, Seamus Hearney from Ireland. He has a delightful impish sense of humour which makes everything fun. He is also quite shy. Every night the Hall was packed for the poetry readings, which was amazing considering the small population. Nearly everyone could speak English. David appeared in the local paper, and his poems were translated into Icelandic.

We were taken on a coach ride with a fascinating guide. We stopped quite often. Once there was time to slip into one of the very warm pools which were everywhere, and very good for health and energy. We also ate some good seaweed, and went to a chapel built in remembrance of a famous poet. We took lots of photos which I treasure.

I was lucky enough to be with Seamus Hearney in the coach, and he made it a laugh-a-minute. Also memorable was the reception given by the President of Iceland, Vigdis Finnbogadotta, a very beautiful woman who spoke movingly in perfect English.

On the last night the poets were all asked to do a little 'turn' other than to read their own poems. Seamus sang a beautiful Irish song, and David read a favourite poem instead of one of his. It was a touching and moving evening. We said goodbye to our Icelandic friends quite sadly, then drove to the airport in the afternoon and, once again, I felt I was driving over the moon's surface. The flight was uneventful but the landing at Heathrow at 10 pm was not much fun because we couldn't find our car; at least not for an hour or two. When we did find it and paid up the £25 it cost, we drove to our hotel at the Devil's Punchbowl. They were all in a state because they said some poisonous environmental substance had leaked into the 'Gents'. We were too tired to get excited about this, so we went straight to our bedroom. We returned to the Island the next morning. After these unusual trips abroad I'm always quite surprised to find that everything is exactly as it was when we went away.

Early October 1985 saw us once more packing up for a *World Poetry Conference,* this time in Corfu. Greece was another place I'd always longed to visit, so I was very excited. Unfortunately the journey had quite a few anxieties.

When we eventually arrived in Athens, which is my most unfavourite Airport, we had a long and anxious wait for a 'plane to Corfu. Apparently David's ticket was alright for the journey, but mine wasn't. We had to wait until everyone boarded the 'plane to see if there was a spare seat for me. David was due to make the opening welcome at the Hilton at 9 am the next day, but he was determined not to leave me at the uncomfortable Airport, bristling with armed guards.

Finally, we were allowed on the 'plane with our luggage, but worse was to come!

A taxi took us to the Hilton, but when we arrived well after midnight the receptionist told is that there was no room for us and we must make our way to another hotel for the night. At this David had one of his rare explosions! He told them that we were guests of the Greek Government, and this was no way to treat us. He demanded to see Mimo Morina, the General Secretary of the World Conference, and the General Manager, AT ONCE! When David draws himself up to his full height of 6ft 3in and uses his effective voice, he is quite scary and fortunately it had the desired effect. In no time at all the organisers arrived and we were soon in a very beautiful suite overlooking the sea and the moon, and best of all eating a tasty champagne supper (courtesy of the Management). So it ended with us having a good laugh.

The next day, when we told our fellow poets about it all, they were astounded. Apparently they had protested too about the lack of accommodation on the first night, but they were firmly directed to a nearby hostel!

From then on the conference went well. David made a good opening speech. The food was excellent and so was the sea. At night there were outdoor banquets, followed by poetry readings and discussions.

One day we all went in a coach around the northern part of Corfu. Larry Durrell's house was pointed out to us. The view of Albania inspired David to write a new poem which he dedicated to Larry. This poem was called 'A Further Frontier', and was published to much acclaim.

We had a few more interesting happenings in 1985. We went off to London for the launching of Paul Ferris' book of Dylan Thomas' letters, and then a very interesting seminar in Plymouth on the subject of dreams, arranged by Bernard Samuels. David introduced a surrealist film by Man Ray. Then R D Laing gave his theories on dreams. Finally, Colin Wilson gave us a very erudite lecture on the brain. There were interesting contributions from Anne Born, Paul Hyland and Alexis Lykiard.

On 10th November 1985 we left quite early to drive to Hartland House to stay with Satish and June Kumar. During the journey David was inspired to write one of his most moving poems called *November in Devon*.

I shall always remember the welcome we had from Satish; he was standing at the front door with his arms wide open, saying *Welcome, Welcome!* We only stayed for one night, but it was perfect in every way! Satish Kumar is another special person, and an inspiration to so many; his attitude to life and love is one I would like to copy. He is one of the few people whose advice I would follow.

Our dear friend Gill Rook gave a fancy dress party to end 1985 in great style. David was Raffles and I was a Pierrot in black and white.

1986

The next year was very fulsome too. 1986 started with snow which lasted until the end of February. A really old-fashioned winter.

When the Spring finally arrived we went to a party given by the Tate Gallery to launch a book of poetry called *With a Poet's Eye.* Many poets had been asked to write a poem about one of their favourite Tate pictures. David chose *Entrance to a Lane* by Graham Sutherland. It was a good poem and a tribute to Graham Sutherland who had illustrated several of David's *Poems 1937-1942.* I enjoyed the party, especially because our friend Stephen Romer was over from Paris and there was a great atmosphere. The book was a sell-out.

In 1986 it was the fiftieth anniversary of the first Surrealist exhibition in England, so some organisers of Kent University decided to have a week's celebration in Canterbury. Duncan Scott invited us to stay in his large house, and we arrived in time for a fulsome welcome from Dr Robert Short on the stage of the University. He spoke of David and Michel Rely in glowing terms. At the supper party afterwards, I met Roger Cardinal, a real charmer, and we had much in common.

The next day many of the students dressed in exotic surrealist costumes, which added to the fun of it all. Tony Penrose, Michel Rely, Sarah Wilson and Mel Gooding all spoke very well about surrealism and David joined the discussion. Stanley William Hayter opened the Exhibition.

When the seminar was over, we were on the road for Ulay in Wiltshire, going from East to West. We found our way quite easily in our Skoda, which used to play-up on every occasion. It was a perfect Summer's evening in May, and the young couple who were organising the poetry reading took us to their home for supper. 'Do you eat animals?' they asked us. We quickly pretended we were vegetarians! The reading went well on a perfect May evening and the Hall was in the heart of the countryside.

The next day we went to stay near Bath with David's Russian friend, Olga Laurence, and her husband George. This is always a special place to stay. David has known Olga since he was a young man, and she is a delightful and perfect hostess.

After all that we only had four weeks at home to prepare for the big World Poetry Congress in Florence. This was worth remembering too.

We flew to Pisa with our dear old friend Miron. Again it wasn't an easy journey because there was a train strike when we got there. After a few hours wait, the organisers said they would send a taxi for us. Just before it arrived, a train pulled in and we went off on it. The hotel was teeming with poets, and the first night banquet was very grand. It was such fun meeting up with all our old friends again, and on a warm June evening. I was able to wear a cool evening gown. I was asked if people changed into evening clothes in England, and of course I said, 'Yes, indeed we do!'

The next day we were taken by coach to a beautiful Monastery, Le San Minatore, where the Festival was to take place. Apparently it is where the Queen Mother comes to rest and enjoy herself. On the coach I sat next to the blue-eyed Ferlinghetti, who made me chuckle about Festival organisers. After the welcome speeches it was lunch time. We sat at tables of eight in a warm courtyard, and enjoyed delicious food, laughter and wine.

This arrangement went on for a week. I used to snooze in the afternoon under a shady tree. The poets were all busy holding seminars. One afternoon President Mitterand arrived. There was virtually no-one to greet him so I arose from my snooze to say welcome, and he kissed my hand and was most gallant. When I told the Congress about it, they were quite jealous. Although I can recall all these events as if they were dreams, I am able to read my diaries for more factual reports.

Anyway, the *9th World Poetry Congress* in Florence was the most lavish we went to. On the last day we were taken by coach to a splendid hotel up in the mountains, and given a ten-course lunch. This was apparently where the Italian Government entertained Royalty and visiting VIPs. The food was really amazing. On the way home in the coach I was stung by a hornet, which sobered me up no end. David and his fellow poets were most concerned, and I was put to bed with pills to sleep off the pain. Thankfully I was well enough to attend the farewell concert. Allen Ginsberg and Gregory Corso played the major part in this.

On our return it was still quite summery for July in England, so we had two months of visitors and friends, and went to the usual busy Cowes Week.

Adam Gadley was coaxed by Simon Callow, the actor, to impersonate David starving in an attic in Paris, by reading some of his diaries for the Edinburgh Festival. We went to a rehearsal of it in London with quite a large audience. It was a strange experience for David. It went down quite well at the Festival, but the reviews said it was a bit too sad and serious.

Soon it was time to be off again. This time to Belgrade for our first time 'behind the Iron Curtain'. We stayed in a huge modern hotel overlooking the Danube. The purpose of the visit was for David to discuss his work with other writers at a Congress. It was a different experience, but most interesting. On the last day all the poets read their work in the Town Square of Belgrade.

We were guests for the last party at Ivan Lalic's, a wonderful translator and poet. This party went on until 4 am when we were returned to our hotel fairly exhausted. We had to be up early for *An English Round Table* session, discussing *The Apocalypse Now.*

Returning to our hotel, we found it was too packed out to get a meal, so we returned to our bedroom and ordered two lunches to be brought up by room service, and we were served in ten minutes. We felt rather pleased with ourselves about that! But we still had to attend another intense last night discussion in the evening.

The next day we flew back to Heathrow without too many hitches, to await a 'plane to Leuven in Belgium for yet another Poetry Congress. This took place at the Irish University and the subject was Le Gouffre (The Abyss). We enjoyed it very much, and I greedily ate plenty of Belgian chocolates.

On the last night I bought a huge gas balloon on which all the poets signed their names, and some wrote a message. We let it off on a starry night and wondered where it would land.

By the time we returned home from all that, it was nearly November. I had to settle down to teaching all my neglected pupils; David did some writing, and my family were pleased to see us safely home. I returned to a Keep Fit class to try to lose a little weight after all that good Belgian food. Then it was Christmas again. Thankfully we didn't have to go abroad again before that.

1987

A sad start for 1987 when Terry Waite was reported missing, and remained in a Beirut prison for over five years.

David's *Self-Discharged* was broadcast on Radio 4. It was a movingly written piece about David's life in Horton Mental Hospital, and I'm glad we have the tape-recording of it. Later, Satish Kumar published it in full, in Resurgence.

Also early in that year I gave a talk at Wellington Middle School, Newport, about *Living with a Poet*. My grandson Jake was in the class. Later, all thirty of the pupils wrote me a description of my talk. It was most enjoyable.

Colin Benford's Bibliography on David was published in March 1987. A handsome hard-back, which will be invaluable for David's researchers. I believe it cost Colin a great deal in time and money, but he is so devoted to David that he took it cheerfully and he's been helping us ever since.

In 1987 the PEN Club were celebrating fifty years since their formation. There was to be much celebrating in Lugano. David was pleased to be asked to give a talk on the environment. Francis King was their President, and he was most gracious to us. Its quite expensive to fly to Switzerland via Milan. The British Council gave us £185, which helped a little. As David doesn't like going alone, he always has to pay for my expensive air ticket. But he does this without any fuss, even if it's tricky sometimes. It was my first visit to Lugano and I enjoyed it very much. I had packed a few smart clothes for the PEN Congress, and I was quite upset when my suitcase was lost at Milan Airport. I was determined not to let it spoil all the fun. Two days later it arrived at the hotel intact! I was able to dress up for the last night, and listen to David delivering his paper on the environment. He had started his talk with a quote from Gerard Manley Hopkins. *Long live the weeds* . . . His paper was later published in *Resurgence*. The closing speech the next day, by Francis King, the PEN President, was memorable. We almost missed the last ferry back to the Island, but we caught it with minutes to spare and arrived home at 10 pm

Two weeks later we were off to London again for David to attend a dinner-party at Burlington House. It was for a gathering of Poets, Writers and Musicians. I wasn't invited, but it gave me great pleasure seeing David go off in his dinner jacket. We stayed with an old boyfriend of mine from the Marlow days, called Alan Morris. It was good to talk to him about the old days. Christine Wild came to have supper with us. David returned around midnight, full of stories about the dinner-party and the good friends that he had met. The next day Mark Gerson, the photographer, arrived at Sussex Gardens, where we stayed, to take plenty of photographs of David. They were all very flattering and have been most useful. Then I drove bravely via the Marble Arch and Hyde Park Corner for lunch with Kathleen Raine. She had cooked us a banquet. We went home via Emsworth to have tea with Annie Goosens, an old friend whom David has known since he was seventeen.

The next day our neighbour died in his garden. He was about to retire from his job as a bus-driver. He told his sister that he didn't feel very well, and he died; as I put it in my diary: *By his pond, surrounded by lilac and syringa, a perfect resting place.* Lila, his sister, was in a bad state but gradually all his family arrived and took over.

The General Election was on 11th June, and apart from voting for the Liberals we took very little interest in it! I continued teaching, and every week I met Charles Loving for our spot called *Poetry Time* on Hospital Radio. Also, I checked up on my old friends, Will and Bertha, both in Residential Homes, and May, still struggling on alone. Two weeks later David gave a reading at the Purcell Room, which was rather uneventful, but we did go to see Brian Peeper, a young Dutch poet fan of David's, who had just bought Roman Blacony for £600, which David had written when only sixteen, and insisted on giving it to David for a present. Luckily, he is very rich.

At the end of June, George Barker and his son Sebastian, came to give a reading at the Apollo Theatre. It was all in celebration of Tennyson's centenary, and ably arranged by Kevin West. Paul Hyland, Jeremy Hooker and Sean Strett also took part.

Early in July 1987, Alan Clodd rang with the exciting news that he had sold some of David's manuscripts to the British Library for £6,000, quite unbelievable! Pam Chandler came to stay for her birthday, so we had two celebrations that day.

Later that month David finished off his introduction for his *Collected Poems,* published by OUP in 1988.

But there was more to do in 1987. A reading at 'Ettys'. On the way to London we often stop at Mel Gooding's, near Richmond, for lunch. He is a good friend and a surrealist Art specialist. He always cooks us a good lunch, and it breaks the journey. We stayed with Alan again in Sussex Gardens, which wasn't far from the reading.

The next day David gave a reading at the Tate Gallery with Jeremy Reed. It was a very good venue for them both.

Home for the inevitable Cowes Week. On 2nd August we listened to David's *Requiem* on Radio 3, set to music by Priaulx Rainier. On 22nd August 1987, we went to Billingham Manor for a ceremony to scatter the ashes of Olivia Manning. Alan Clodd came down from London; Neville and June were there, and the Lawrences organised lunch for us all. The ashes were put to rest in a stone receptacle in the garden. Neville read one of Olivia's letters. David read his *Gravel-Pit Field,* Helen Miller-Smith read extracts from the *Balkan Trilogy,* and I read *Remember* by Christina Rosetti. Michael Lawrence and Francis King spoke movingly of Olivia's life. Beryl Bainbridge and James Cameron's widow were there too. We had a delicious lunch with plenty of wine to toast Olivia's memory. Neville Braybrooke is now finishing her biography. Alan stayed the night with us and I persuaded him to come for a swim with me at Gurnard Bay. He stayed for a few days more, and was helpful with sorting our David's endless papers. We sent Bob up into the attic, but we couldn't find anything of David's up there for Alan to publish.

Sebastian Barker asked David to write the introduction to Elizabeth Smart's collected poetry. He did this without any fuss, and quite quickly.

It was a memorable autumn, with the famous gales of 1987 which did so much damage. I had some very good news on 3rd November - my divorce arrangements had left me the big house, *Westport,* at Yarmouth. My daughter-in-law, Sheena, was living there with her three children but she wanted to live in a smaller house since her separation from my son. The house was put on the market and, although it was a perfect family house, many of the bids fell through so we were getting desperate. I decided to apply for planning permission to have three bungalows built in the large garden. To my surprise Sheena, who was working at the George Hotel in Yarmouth, managed to clinch a deal with some builders and so it was soon arranged. I was able to buy a house that she liked in Newport, pay the Capital Gains Tax, and have a nice little sum to invest. For the first time in my life money wasn't a problem. So we did a bit of celebrating, but I hated it when I saw Westport being systematically knocked down by bulldozers.

Another nice thing happened, Flissy had a daughter on 23rd November and so Milo is now the father of two beautiful girls, Poppy and Rosie. To celebrate all this we were off at the end of November for a few nights with the Harveys at Westminster Abbey. David had been asked to read at St James, Piccadilly, again. We always enjoy staying with Julian and Anthony Harvey. It is a perfect place to stay in London, but it was only for three days this time. I drove bravely to Golders Green for supper with David's friends the Nadals. David is a very good navigator, and has a good map of London in his head.

The Tate told David that they had bought the collage he made in the 50s from a private owner, and that it was going on show.

I also had a little lift when Chris Turner came to see us and wanted to print my journal of 1944 for his book called *Marlow Station.* This was published in November 1987 and it highlighted Marlow in the War, my diary and various comments about the call-up of women to be signal-women. It had been an interesting period in my life. It was good to have it in book form and its been invaluable for me when I'm asked endlessly to talk of my experiences as a Signalwoman for the GAR at Marlow Station. I average about seven talks a year still, which is quite an achievement since I started in 1962 using the title *Life begins at 40,* and now it's *Growing old Gratefully.*

When I had about twenty-five private pupils to teach, I used to take them on outings at the end of every term. Sandown Zoo, Carisbrooke Castle, Osborne House, and of course to a Pantomime every Christmas. Strangely we never took ourselves to Havenstreet, where the Island has a perfect old-fashioned railway line, complete with signal box. One day I'll go there, even if it has to be in a wheelchair!

I started my 1987 diary by saying 'I have a feeling that this is going to be an exciting and prosperous year'. Then I add in brackets, '. . . in spite of being £45,000 overdrawn at the Bank!' This was because the money for Westport didn't come through for quite a time and I had to buy a bridging loan to buy Sheena a house. This is a very bad idea moneywise, but it all worked out very well in the end, especially as I didn't have to pay any Estate Agent's fee for the sale.

In order to write an accurate account of our world travels, I am having to recount each year as my diary has recorded the events. This may not make very interesting reading, but I fear it needs to be done. I am at last up to 1988, and so I have only ten more years to go. I'm intrigued about the ending of an autobiography! My father wrote his diary the day he died. I want to finish this before I die, so that I can enjoy reading it! I hope you will too, dear readers, as they used to say in the old days! I am very touched by the support I get from David and also my family and friends.

1988

So here we are in 1988, and I note the following: the gales and rain in January made our roof leak, so the bed had to be moved. Years later we had enough money to pay for the roof to be redone and the ceiling mended.

In 1988, I note that David gave several readings, but the chief excitement was our visit to Malmö in Sweden in the merry month of May. This led to all sorts of good things.

After giving a reading in the Purcell Room with Kathleen Raine in April, chiefly for the launching of David's *Collected Poems,* we received an invitation from LARS to join a world Poetry Congress in Malmö, Sweden. I was asked to read for Kathleen Raine, who didn't feel well enough to attend. They sent us out flight tickets, which made for an easy journey. Even so, we managed to get on the wrong hydrofoil to Malmö, but all was easily resolved as usual and after changing into a cool dress at our Hotel, we were swiftly driven to a theatre. I had to be on the stage with David. I read some of Kathleen Raine's stories about Humphrey Jennings, and David answered questions from a very attentive audience. The whole evening was dedicated to the life and film works of Humphrey Jennings.

The next day we were all welcomed by the Mayor of Malmö at the Town Hall. David was delighted to meet Octavio Paz again. The poet, Adonis, was his charming self and very encouraging about my reading of Kathleen Raine's poems. Sweden was having a freak heatwave, with temperatures in the mid-eighties, and so it was good to go in coaches to their mini-Stonehenge by the sea, the next day. After exploring the stones we all got together in an old house for lunch, and the playing of classical music by a quartet. We were driven speedily back to Malmö, where I was told that I had to 'chair' a meeting about Blake. Two learned professors spoke about him in Swedish to a crowded audience in the Town Hall, and I was nudged when it was time for me to read *Songs of Innocence.* I was a bit bewildered by all this, until it dawned on me that I was really taking on the role of Kathleen Raine.

The following day the readings took place in a large disused Railway Station. It had a banner across the platform which said: *God's Expedition,* but we weren't sure of the explanation. Again there was a huge audience, but fortunately the microphones were good. I was on first to read Kathleen Raine's poems, and these were read again in Swedish by an actress. The same thing happened for David when he read. He had a book of his poems translated into Swedish before we went to Malmö. The final performance was by Octavio Paz, who received a standing ovation. Due to the freak heatwave there was a dramatic thunderstorm at the end of the concert, which engrossed us all.

Two days later we were off to Paris, staying in a large room at the Hotel St Pierre. This was paid for by a fund that the trustees of a French translator had arranged. It had been decided to ask David to be the first guest because the young man had translated many of David's poems. He had tragically died of a mystery illness at the age of thirty.

While we were in Paris, Christine Jordis gave a party for us. We also went to the Surrealist AGM with Georgette Camille, after which some of us had a supper party at the Select.

As a coincidence, I discovered that Daniel Rotten was living very near out hotel. He had stayed with us in Yarmouth in the 1960s to learn English. It was great to discover that he had become an eminent gynaecologist. We had many memories to catch up with. He used to be so rude about my French! In the 1960s I stayed with his father, who was an Haute Couturier. He offered me one of his outfits for £12, but at the time I couldn't afford it!

Also in June we went to London to give an outdoor reading at Burlington House, sponsored by SOX.

Because of my connection with Sweden, I was invited to teach forty-five Swedish students for six weeks at Freshwater. This was my first experience of teaching foreign students, and I loved it. They were so keen to learn, and especially to visit Tennyson's house.

They told me that his poem, *Ring out Wild Bells,* was read every New Year's Eve in Sweden. They were also fascinated by Queen Victoria's Osborne House.

This ritual of teaching students went on for five years every June or July. They paid me generously, and it kept me in touch with young people. I regret that I'm too old and crippled to do it now.

In 1988 David's bust by Gertrude Hermes was bought for the National Portrait Gallery. We were sorry that we weren't free to go to the reception for that, but it was time to be off for the Edinburgh Festival. David had been asked to give a paper there on Francis Peekaboo, and he took quite a time preparing it.

It was a long drive to undertake in our erratic Skoda, but we managed. We stopped in Manchester to have tea with the Freers. He had been head of sixth-form education, and David and I had been up twice visiting his top classes and answering questions on Surrealism and poetry. They had just returned from the Edinburgh Festival, and they were full of it. We had arranged to have supper with David's nephew and wife, Ted and Margaret, who were having a birthday party for their eight-year old daughter Claire. Joan Gascoyne, from San Francisco, was there too, so it was quite a celebration. We didn't think too much of our hotel, and were glad to be on the road again.

Once I had tackled the six lanes out of Manchester, it was easy going and we found our hotel by tea-time in a crowded Edinburgh.

Richard Calvocoressi fetched us for a concert in the Gallery of Modern Art, and there was a very lively party for us to join after that.

The next day was Sunday and we went to celebrate my brother Ben's seventieth birthday party at a large hotel a few miles out of Edinburgh. Ben and Joan's son and daughter-in-law, Patrick and Pippy, live in Edinburgh so we were quite a family party. When the lunch was over we were dropped off at a Gallery to see Lucien Freud's exhibition.

The next morning we went to a good Fringe event about the life of Anna Markham. After a rest we went to the Art Gallery again at 6 pm with Richard, for David's talk on Peekaboo. This went down very well, and eight of us went out to dinner afterward at an Indian Restaurant.

The next day we had to change hotels because David had been unexpectedly asked to give a talk and reading that Mr de Marco had arranged. We met in a disused Chapel, and there were many others taking part. Richard de Marco is the unauthorised director of Edinburgh Festival, and quite a character.

The five hundred miles back to the Island went easily, but we had to stop one night in Market Yarborough.

A few weeks at home came next. Patrick von Richthofen came to stay. He is a great nephew of the famous pilot in the 1st World War, the Red Baron, and he is busy writing about Henry Miller and Lawrence Durrell at the Villa Seurat, Paris. At 6ft 4in and with perfect manners, he was a guest whom we much enjoyed.

At the end of September we were off to London again for two very pleasant invitations. One was to help celebrate Eileen Agar's eightieth birthday party and to launch her autobiography. She was an artist friend of David's from the early days of Surrealism and a most attractive woman.

The other party was for a retrospective event for Henry Moore at Burlington House. This was a very grand affair and Margaret Thatcher, looking as if she had spent all day in a beauty salon, made a very fulsome speech about her love of Henry Moore's work. I didn't really believe this, and was glad when she finished. We were thankful to be treated to good champagne and food afterwards.

Finally, in October 1988 we were bidden to Dartington Hall in Devonshire, for a good weekend arranged by Kathleen Raine as a tribute to *Temenos,* which she started a few years ago. We spent nearly a week indulging in many cultural events - Philip Sherrard talked on the *Sacredness of Art* and Kathleen Raine on

Poetry and Prophecy. David read with Jeremy Reed; James Cowan talked about the Aborigines; Thetis Blacker showed us her wonderful Batik Work; John Tavener introduced us to his singers, and on the last night we paid tributes to Kathleen Raine at a Gala Dinner, and the evening finished with some famous Indian singers.

After all that we went to stay with Olga and George Lawrence at Brocken End, Bath. By then we had both caught heavy colds so we were not very good guests, but we did go to Gertrude Hermes' daughter's, by the Severn Bridge, for lunch.

We were both glad to be home, but we were told by our doctor that we had been overdoing it. Even so, we had to go to London again following John Tavener's invitation to hear his concert at Westminster Abbey to celebrate a thousand years of Russian Religion. There was a reception afterwards given by the Dean and the Bishop of Winchester. David and John Tavener have a good rapport.

Finally, we had Jean-Claude Masson and his beautiful partner, Anike, to spend Christmas with us. They arrived from Paris about 6 pm laden with wine, champagne and goodies to eat. It was a very special Christmas that year. We all went to spend Christmas Day with Sue and Miles. They cope so well with so many of us. The next day was the family hockey match. For the 3rd day of Christmas I gave a turkey dinner here and Sue and Jenny came to help. We played all sorts of silly games.

The next day Jean-Claude and Anike left for Truro in their car. I think they really enjoyed an English Christmas, and David enjoyed speaking French most of the time. For us it ended 1988 very nicely!

Photographs

My mother Lorna Slocock at 21, one of 11 children of Rev. Slocock
& Emily of Mottisfont

My Father, Guy Tyler

Edward, Judy and Ben, my brothers and me

Edward, Judy and Ben, my brothers and me - slightly later

End Farm, Buckinghamshire, where I was born

David & I on our wedding day in 1975

Alan Clodd, David's publisher for many years

Neville Braybrooke, Edward Upward, David. Three men of letters.

Allen Ginsberg and David in New York

Lawrence Durrell pondering with us in his kitchen

A group of us enjoying lunch during Lawrence Durrell's seminar in Avignon

David in 1979 in the garden at Northwood

Christine Jordis, David's French translator

Olivier Poivre d'Arvor
Conseiller Culturel près l'Ambassade de France
Directeur de l'Institut Français du Royaume-Uni
et Madame Olga Poivre d'Arvor

prient Monsieur et Madame David Gascoyne
de bien vouloir venir à la cérémonie
le Jeudi 27 Juin à 18ʰ 00

R. S. V. P.
0171-838 2058

Institut Français
15 Queensberry Place, SW7

The invitation for the 'Chevalier dans l'Ordre National des Arts et Lettres'

Olivier Poivre d'Arvor welcoming us to the award of the 'Chevalier'

Our Silver Wedding Anniversary picture

The Bronze of David by Gertrude Hermes, 1956, in the National Portrait Gallery

1989

1989 started well with a reading in Nottingham. We enjoyed going to see all
the haunts of D H Lawrence. We had a pleasant drive home via the Harmers of
the Stratford days, and we also stayed with my brother at Marlow for a
weekend on the way home. But for me the most memorable part of the year
was our visit to PARIS! David had been invited by Cecil and Lil Michaelis, to
write an introduction to her work in an art catalogue, and to go to the opening
of her *vernissage*. We flew off on a chilly June day but, almost as soon as we
arrived, Paris was having a real heatwave. I decided I must find myself an
attractive sundress in the Boulevard St Michel. I hadn't expected it to be such
a delightful experience. I went into quite a big dress shop and was soon
surrounded by ladies whose one desire was to find me a dress that would
really suit me. They were pleased with my halting French, and in no time at all
I discovered a dress of my dreams - beautifully cut in black and white, and
with a hemline that quite disguised the worst parts of my figure. When I told
them that I was off for a special lunch with my husband, they were touchingly
delighted! I left the shop feeling like a Paris model, and the dress was the
equivalent of £30 in English money. For the next five years no other dress
seemed as cool or as elegant. Sadly, I'm too fat for it now, but it was an
experience I will never forget. That week in Paris in the hot sunshine was one
of the best holidays we've ever had. We dined with many of David's friends,
and we enjoyed watching all the Paris preparations for the 200 year
celebrations of the French Revolution.

As soon as we were home, I had to teach the Swedish students for six weeks,
and earn myself some money.

On the 29th July 1989, we were invited to the wedding of George Barker and
Elspeth, near Cromer in Norfolk. I'm not all that keen on weddings, but this
was very special. To begin with, George and Elspeth had been waiting a long
time before they could marry. They had a Catholic service in a little church in
Sheringham. Elspeth looked beautiful, and when they were actually married
we all clapped. Back at Bintry House, all the guests had been invited to bring a
bottle and a plate of food, and it took place in their garden. There were dozens
of children playing around, and I enjoyed the way George handled them all.
They obviously adored him, and he is the worthy father of at least twelve. In
between amusing them, he talked with John Heath-Stubbs and his other
poetic friends and writers. I have some good photos of them all. Sebastian had
the sulks! This was because he wanted me to share in his excitement of having
fallen seriously in love. When I prosaically asked him about his wife and
children, he told me I was 'A prudish old bore', or words to that effect! He also
chastised David, but I think it was mostly the champagne talking. Now that he

is so happily married to Hilary Davies, the girl of his dreams, I realize that at last he had found a serious partner.

I know there were some good speeches by the Barnard brothers at the reception, and the whole atmosphere was so genuine, entirely different from the awful expensive weddings that we are forced to attend sometimes. Elspeth and George had a honeymoon in Italy.

Also in July we went to the celebrations at Salisbury Cathedral School, where David had been a chorister for five years. It was good to watch him talking with all his old school friends, and we had our photograph taken in a group. During the supper held in the Bishop's Palace, David read his *Sarum Sestina* which he had written for Satish Kumar. It was all about schooldays at Salisbury, and it went down well.

In September we were off to the King's Lynn annual Festival of Literature, sponsored by Armagnac. I mention this because it was plentifully donated, and some of the younger poets drank too much before their readings! Gavin Ewart was a totally charming host and sang as well as read his poetry. Also, George Barker was there in his wheelchair, and my favourite, Ursula Fanthorpe. There was a good atmosphere all the time. The BBC recorded most of it. We stayed in Walshingham with a solicitor and his wife. We drove in every day past Sandringham. Lady Fermoy, Princess Diana's grandmother, attended every session, and was a generous and charming patron. Once again, I decided that Norfolk would be a county where I would like to live! But that's an ambition not be fulfilled.

October of 1989 was quite busy with the launching of *Novalis* at the Quay Arts Centre. Stephen Stuart-Smith, of Enitharmon Press had invited us both to read there.

Then it was off to London again for a celebratory lunch at the Swiss Embassy. This was because David had written a review of the work of one of the leading Swiss writers *Cingria*. I much enjoyed the company and the food, and the sheer excellence of it all. It turned out that the Swiss Ambassador's wife had been taught by my wonderful Miss Bird from Beneden. We then had a good hour with Christine Wild before regirding our loins for a Swiss reception of talks and readings, and plenty of food and wine.

In November we awaited a call from Paris for the launching of David's *Miserere,* a bi-lingual edition of selected poems compiled by François Xavier Jaujard, the editor of Granit Press.

On 9th November 1989, the Berlin Wall came down much to everyone's rejoicing. It was good to watch on television.

On 16th November 1989 we flew to Paris from Eastleigh Airport, and Francois Xavier was at De Gaulle Airport to meet us. We celebrated our arrival with a lavish dinner with Jacqueline de Roux, who had invited Christine Jordis and Sasha, and Kathleen Raine was there too. It was an enchanting evening, but we were glad to get back to our favourite hotel room by 1 am.

Kathleen was staying in a hotel nearby, so we spent much of the time with her. We were also fetched by Bruce van Barthold in his car to spend a day in their house on the outskirts of Paris. Biddy Romer and her six-year-old son joined us for lunch. Later she drove us back to our hotel, and then we went to a French film *La Verité* together. I am recalling this Paris trip in detail because it was virtually the last one we had. My diaries are very useful. The launching of *Miserere* kept on being delayed, due to printing troubles, so we decided to go to stay with Larry Durrell in Sommières.

We flew from Paris to Marseilles and then a friend took us to our hotel in Aix-en-Provence. Patrick Hutchinson arrived with a bottle of the new Beaujolais. After we had demolished the wine, we went to a very elegant fish restaurant and made plans for the drive to Sommières on the morrow.

The flower market was close to the hotel, so we went in search of flowers for Françoise, who was celebrating her birthday with a large lunch party in Larry's house. I enjoyed the drive down with Patrick and his beautiful partner Nikke. She let me practice my French on her during the three hour drive. When we arrived at Larry's old house, we were greeted like long-lost relatives. The drink flowed, and it was a sit-down lunch for twenty-four of us. I was lucky enough to sit next to Larry, and I shamelessly flirted with him. I love the respect and deep affection he shows to David. There was a wood fire burning in our bedroom, which was very cosy, and I had a little snooze up there before the excitement of the evening. When I went down the next day at 6 am for our ritual cup of tea, Larry was in the kitchen drinking white wine. He persuaded me to join him and we had an enchanting conversation. I felt like a teenager again, and quite forgot David's early morning cuppa.

We had a little shopping spree in Sommières and then Françoise invited us to her part of the house to watch a film that had recently been made with Henry Miller, with Larry and Alfred Perlès as the stars.

Soon it was time to go off to the *Quatres Vents* for lunch. Larry wanted me to drive his car, but I couldn't manage the gears so he drove, and I was able to drink as much wine as I wanted. Mary Hadkinson joined us for lunch, which was typically French and delicious.

At about 4.30, one of the guests drove us to Aix. We tried to find Patrick's house near Aix but failed, so we were dropped off at our hotel. When Patrick arrived to take us out to dinner, I was feeling too tired to join them and settled for bed and a snack in the bedroom.

The next day we flew back to Paris with a 'plane full of Japanese. I had quite a thrill when over the intercom a message came that a car was awaiting Mr and Mrs Gascoyne at the Airport. It was the faithful François Xavier who took us back to our hotel, packed up all our things and took us to the De la Vigne Hotel, close by and with plenty of character. We were up on the fifth floor. The adjoining bathroom had French windows onto a balcony. It was old-fashioned and much to our liking. We discovered a good restaurant opposite called 'La Cambouse', where we lunched every day with different friends. It was such a busy week awaiting the launching of *Miserere* on 6th December. We were invited to the Palais Royale with all the Irish Poets for a reception organised by the French Cultural Minister, Jacques Leng. This was as good as going to Buckingham Palace as far as I was concerned! Later we had an hilarious lunch at a French Pub with John Montague and all the Irish Poets.

At last 6th December arrived with all the copies of David's *Miserere*. We had several consultations with Odile of Village Voice, where the launching was to take place. David's poet friends and translators arrived at our hotel for last minute consultations. The Village was packed when we arrived. I was glad that I'd had a Parisian hair-do, and had put on my best long dress. It all went so well with many tributes to David, and long queues of friends wanting a signed edition of the book.

Later, Christine Jordis had organised a reception at her house for all our close friends with plenty to eat and drink. Unfortunately, David was feeling quite ill by then with the start of a wretched 'flu bug. So we had to be taken back to the hotel by taxi before the party ended.

When we arrived at the hotel the lift had broken down, so we had to slowly mount the large staircase as far as the fifth floor. I was really worried for David's health. There was no let up for the next day - François Xavier drove us to his house in Paris and relentlessly asked David to sign about fifty copies of his books. At last we were driven to Charles de Gaulle Airport to catch our little plane back to Eastleigh Airport. There we took a taxi to the ferry and then another taxi home to Cowes.

The house was bitterly cold and I discovered, to my dismay, that I had left my black bag with all its helpful medicines and hot water bottle at the Airport in Eastleigh.

The next day my helpful Sue came to the rescue and sorted it all out. We were both quite ill with 'flu. I foolishly struggled on with an outing to a Pantomime with my pupils, and even worse to read poems at Newtown Church for the

Christmas Service for Hospital Radio. By Monday I was worse, and David was better, so he had to get up to help me.

Happily by Christmas-time we were both better and able to join in the family fun.

At last 1989 came to a close. It had been a year *plus chargée* as the French say.

1989

1990

In 1990, on February 17th, David organised a concert at the Apollo Theatre in aid of Dr Baksi's new diabetic premises. It was called *A Programme of Green and Evergreen Poetry*. Joy and Francis Hall agreed to read with us, and we used to go to their house in Ryde to rehearse. The evening went really well and Dr Baksi introduced it. The theatre was full and, thanks to raffles and refreshments, we made £200 for the diabetic clinic, and he gave us all a charming note of thanks. I was pleased for David's sake that the evening was a success because it brought him out of his inertia.

A week later it was my turn to be self-indulged. Sue and I went off to the Forestmere Health Farm for a long weekend, and thus another pipe-dream was fulfilled! It was good mixing with the rich and famous. We had a strict but delicious diet, an attractive bedroom, breakfast in bed, lots of brisk walks, warm swims, massages, lectures and bike rides. The weekend flew by and we left feeling very fit, both having lost three pounds in weight and £300 in money! I wouldn't want to go again, but it is certainly my idea of a good holiday. David coped very well all by himself.

When the May Bank Holiday arrived, we were off to the Hay-on-Wye Festival. We stayed at a farm house about a mile out of town. Hay itself was alive with Festival goers, and I have never seen so many bookshops. The organiser was generous and helpful. and we soon knew what we had to do. It was glorious weather. David read with a Romanian Lady poet called Nina Cassian. She had a great sense of humour. We met dozens of old friends and listened to many poets and writers, one of my favourites being Frank Muir. Roger McGough was good too. It is impossible to include everyone. Brenda Ross came over to join in, as did Penny Durrell and her husband. They both live within twenty miles of Hay-on-Wye.

After five days of intensive festive cheer, we were off to stay with Brenda and Steve Ross at Herb Cottage, Shyborry Green. They were so hospitable and took us everywhere. We were quite sad to leave, but we had an arrangement to stay one night with Penny Durrell. This was most enjoyable too. It was good to discuss Larry with Penny. She has much of his charm, and some of his bite too. Their cottage was so beautiful, covered in pink roses, and delphiniums everywhere. It was a most pleasant week away.

A few days later it was London again for David's reading at the Poetry Society, and various other events. I have lost my 1990 diary, so I'm having to stretch my brain fiercely for memories. If I wait until it's found, I may never be able to finish this memoire.

Early in October 1990 we went to a most interesting conference in Madrid relating to the Spanish Civil War, and very well arranged by John England of the British Institute.

A plaque was unveiled paying tribute to five British writers who lost their lives fighting Franco. David read one of Stephen Spender's poems. Iris Murdoch and John Bayley flew over for the occasion.

Professors Pring Mill and Valentine Cunningham spoke most eloquently about the Civil War in Spain. They answered many questions from students. Rafael and Jacinth Nadal entertained us at their orangery, situated in the middle of Madrid. It was a week to remember.

Towards the very end of 1990 on December 27th, we flew to Paris to stay near Anike and Jean-Claude Masson, in order to see the New Year arrive in Paris. (Another wish of mine!). We were able to explore Paris, visit friends and go to art museums in the day-time. In the evenings Anike and Jean-Claude fetched us by car and we had delicious long French dinners with them and their friends

On New Year's Eve, we had the most enormous feast which started with oysters and ended with chocolate truffles. We drank too much champagne and arrived back at the hotel at about 2 am in the morning.

1991

New Year's day was spent with Bruce Van Barthold and Joanne with their new baby, Theo. But on 2nd January 1991, whilst we were lunching at a very posh restaurant, the *Fin Gourmet,* with Christine Jordis, I was suddenly overcome by a terrible nausea. I only had time to stumble to a very public basin where I was violently sick. David and Christine were most concerned. They ordered me a taxi and rang the hotel where I was helped up to the bedroom by a kind chambermaid who put me into bed and found me a hot water bottle! Later, David returned and he went swiftly to a pharmacy to tell them of my troubles. The French have wonderful pills for excessive sickness and nausea, called Oxyboldine, so I was soon feeling better. The next morning we were hoping to have lunch with Edmond Jabès, the writer, but when we rang his wife she said, 'Il est mort', and David was able to comfort her a little. We telephoned to England so that the Press could organise obituaries about Edmond Jabès. On January 3rd we had been invited to a very special dinner party by Anne Wade Minowski. By that time I was feeling quite ill again. David made a great effort to go, but after two hours he was returned by taxi with violent sickness. So there we were, in our hotel bedroom lying side by side in a big double bed, feeling very ill! Quite comical really! The Maitre d'hôtel sent up a supply of our famous Oxyboldines, and we slept all day and all night, until it was time for the long journey home. That was the second time that we have had to leave Paris feeling really ill, but it hasn't put us off in the least!

Luckily, the first three months were comparatively peaceful, but I did put ten children in for the Ryde Festival verse-speaking classes. I also went in for the adult competitions, but apart from impromptu speaking, I didn't do very well. Also, one of my favourite nieces, Joanna Lewis, had a very lavish wedding in March at Redbourne, to which all the family went. As weddings go, it was a really good one.

On April 7th we flew off again to Toronto for a huge Poetry and Literary Festival, organised by Greg Gatenby. We arrived on one of the hottest April days (80F) in living memory. Our hotel was fantastic, and so was the party in the Hospitality Room with Alan Jenkins, Vernon Scannell, Archie Markham, Seth Vickram, and Kevin Crossley-Holland et al. The hotel provided swimming pools and saunas and breakfasts in bed. The next day David was on the Canadian Radio answering questions, and talking about the Festival. His cousins in Vancouver heard him and rang us up later. The days passed all too quickly. It was bright and sunny but with a very strong cold wind all the time. Mrs Elliot, a local rich friend of the Festival, took us off in her big car to a modern art exhibition, and then to her house. David and I went to Kim's house because she was writing a book about Elizabeth Smart, and wanted to ask David all about her.

On the third day we were all taken by coach to Niagara Falls, which impressed us very much. The evening concert was crowded for David's reading.
John Montague, my favourite Irish poet, also took part. We flew home during the night and a taxi met us at Gatwick, so we were home by 10 am — jet-lagged.

Towards the end of April we went up to the London Museum for the launching of a most complicated book by Nicholas Hagger, called *The Fire and The Stones*. David, Kathleen and Lord Briggs introduced it. We were treated to a lavish dinner at the Barbican Restaurant. Marion came with us and we stayed at her cosy flat. The next day we lunched with Kathleen Raine and Mary Trevelyan before returning home.

In May we were off to Totleigh Barton again. Jeremy Reed was the poet in residence and I remember that he and I had a row after we had finished off a bottle of red wine. He told me that all the poets at the Canadian Poetry Festival were rubbish. This made me so angry with him! He told me that I had no taste in poetry, and had no right to have married David. I then retreated to tell all this to David who, in his gentle way, calmed me down. At the dinner party afterwards, Jeremy had completely forgotten the whole incident, and was all sweetness and light. He introduced David most extravagantly, and it was a very good evening.

We were home in time for a very special visit from Jane and Philip Marsh. Philip and David had been good friends in their young days in Paris. They hadn't met for fifty-eight years, so it was a poignant meeting. I recall they generously came with two bottles of champagne and smoked salmon for lunch, so we had quite a 'frolic' as Philip used to call it. Philip paid great tribute to David on a BBC programme in 1995. Very sadly he died in December 1998. A very remarkable and lovely man.

Another friend of David's came to stay in June 1990, Michael Wishart, with his boy-friend, Tim. Michael is an artist, and had lived life to the full. He and David were very close. He is a wonderful raconteur and has known everyone! Sadly, he too died about three years ago. If there is an after-life, we will be able to have some great parties! I find it sad writing about all our special friends who have died. [This year, 1999, David's very close friend, Yves de Bayser, died, and that saddened David very much. He was the first French poet I had met, and he treated me with such elegance when we first met in Paris.]

Another pleasant event in June 1991 was when we went to help Satish Kumar celebrate twenty-five years of his editorship of *Resurgence*. Three hundred of us met in a huge marquee in the grounds of Hardwich House. Tributes to

Satish came from far and wide, and we all enjoyed a delicious lunch. It was a very happy occasion.

In July 1991 I finished teaching the Swedish Students for the last time. I was quite sad about this. We had a good time at Osborne House, the Farringford, and a residential home in Freshwater. I also organised a good 'fun' party in Milo's woods for all my own pupils. When I look back on these parties, I'm really glad that I took the trouble to have them.

In August we were off to stay with Wayland and Jeanot, who live in an old house in the south of France. It is deep in the country. The weather was perfect and so all meals were out of doors under a huge tree. Wayland is quite a perfectionist in all he does, especially cooking. They had charmingly arranged many parties for us. Jeanot took us up to the top of Mont Ventoux in his car. The view was marvellous. The Tour de France cycle race often includes this route. Jean-Pierre Colombi came from Marseilles to stay the night, and it was good to see him again.

Under the influence of very good French wine, I found the conversation easy to keep up with. We only stayed for a week, but it seemed longer. David had no reading commitments, so it was like a real holiday.

This was our second visit staying with them, and it was most enjoyable.

Back to the Island again for August and September. Early in October 1991 we were off for what was virtually our last International World Poetry Congress. This time it took place in Crete, but we flew to Athens first for a big reception to meet all the other poets and delegates. The next day we had a very early short flight to Crete, but a long wait for coaches to take us the twenty miles to our hotel from Hania to Rithymna. Finally we were all put in taxis. It was worth the wait because our hotel was perfect. There was time for a quick warm swim before the banquet lunch. Then to a conference room where, once more, David had to be on the platform while the lengthy welcomes were given, and Mimo Morina outlined the week's events.

Our bedroom was almost on the beach, and hearing the waves gave me a vivid dream, wherein I was swimming to every country in the world to give them a message of peace! After our delicious Greek yoghurt breakfast we were ready for a busy day. David was in charge of a discussion called *Poetry and the Environment*.

Then a chosen few were driven to have lunch with a Greek Bishop and his nuns. This was a good experience, and we were privileged to be invited.

In the evening David had to preside over another meeting. I made friends with a beautiful Danish model called Anya. The Greek Cultural Minister was in love with her, and it caused a bit of a hassle. After lots of swims with her we were off to a huge outdoor concert for a tribute to the Greek Poet, George Seferis. After that there was a farewell dinner by a pool. We sang Greek songs and danced, so bed was very late.

Quite a busy day!

Our last day was taken up with a press conference, then a coach to the Airport, where the painter Johnny Craxton came all the way to see us and to have a very quick chat. When we arrived in Athens, David was whisked away for a television appearance. Anya and I had to find our way to the Argonaut, the boat which was to take us on a cruise. We changed quickly and met up with David at the huge Athens open-air theatre for an evening of words and music. Alan Bates read some Shakespeare very well; Fanny Ardent read Rimbaud's *Le Bateau Ivre,* his most famous poem. It was the centenary of Rimbaud's death at a Hospital in Marseilles. The acoustics were marvellous. We were welcomed by the Greek Government. This made a late return to our cabin on the boat, and there were gale warnings by then! However, exhaustion overtook us both and we slept the night away. The sun was streaming into our large stateroom cabin when we awoke for breakfast, and to hear about the cruise and the day's excitements.

A TV crew had attached themselves to us, so we were taken to Epidaurus which had a huge 2,000 year old amphitheatre, so that all the poets could be televised reading their poetry. Anya was in charge of them but it was a film for the Greek Government, so we never saw it.

That night, on board the Argonaut, there was a banquet and all the poets read a short poem, after which we did some Greek dancing all around the tables. Bed was very late that night!

No rest the next day, as we went in police convoy to Delphi where, thousands of years ago, Greek civilisation began. It was a wonderful experience and I felt as if I had moved back into the past. In the evening we were off on the cruise again, and passing through the very narrow Corinth canal. We all cheered and drank champagne when our Captain safely navigated our huge ship through! Back to Athens early in the morning to quite a cloudy bleak day, and a long wait at my least favourite Airport. Philip Sherrard was going to meet us there because he lives not too far away. He didn't turn up. and we learned later that his car had broken down in the mountains. So it was a long tiring wait for our 'plane, which was late. When they tried to evict us from our first-class seats, David again came to the fore, telling the stewards that we were guests of the Greek Government and we had no intention of moving. We were very well treated after that.

It was nice to be met at Heathrow with our booked taxi for Portsmouth. Later, Kevin met us at Fishbourne and we returned home at last. Barbara and Peter

Watson had completed some home-decorating before our return, so it was good to return to our spick-and-span home, and to Jeffrey our cat.

A few days later, David celebrated his seventy-fifth birthday on October 10th 1991. We had been invited to Salisbury Cathedral School for the occasion. The pupils arranged a singing of 'Happy Birthday' and then David and I were given a class-room each to talk about poetry. This was much to my liking as I am never happier than when in charge of a class of children. Later they all wrote essays about out visit. In the evening the headmaster had organised an adult dinner party for David, ending with a candle-lit birthday cake. He also paid a tribute to David, saying he was one of their most famous pupils! Then at the end of October there was another poetry festival at Colchester. This time we stayed with David's cousin, Mick Mares and his wife Mavis. They lived about twenty miles out of Colchester, so we drove in for the day's events. Touchingly, after David's reading another birthday cake was produced with the usual fulsome speeches. Kathleen Raine gave a paper on Blake, Jeremy Reed, Joe Allard, Patricia Scanlan and Tony Ellis all took part in the celebrations. Finding our way back to Boxford in the dark, late at night, was horrible.

The next day Jack Barker invited is to his beautiful house near Lavenham, for a relaxing lunch and then a little tour around the Suffolk villages.

Very sadly George Barker, poet, died on 27th October 1991. He was a great character and a wonderful poet.

Early in November, Lucien Jenkins arrived with David's *Collected Journals 1936-1942*, which Skoob books had published. They had an introduction from Kathleen Raine. David was a little dissatisfied with the publicity arrangements, and no reviews had appeared. However, we were pleased to have the Journals all in one volume.

On 18th November 1991, Terry Waite was released and I wrote a tribute to him.

In November 1991 we were invited to a conference in Luxembourg. Mimo Morina wanted poets from all over Europe to come to the Senate House to discuss *The State of Literature after the fall of the Berlin Wall.* So off we flew.

I was impressed with the huge Conference Hall, and the fact that we were ushered to our seats by young men in tails, wearing white gloves. The conference went on for two days, and David made a spirited intervention.

The Russians had plenty to say and they rather took over the meetings. As usual no definite conclusion came of it, but we did send off a resolution to the United Nations. There were the usual lavish receptions, but it was really nice to spend an evening with Pierre Rother at his house with his family. Our return home from Luxembourg Airport was positively luxurious. The waiting rooms provide you with full-size sun-beds, so different from the cramped facilities offered by other airports.

It was good to be back from our last visit of the year abroad. Sadly, on 1st December our beloved cat Jeffrey, had to be put to sleep by Michael. He was suffering from severe liver damage. We had enjoyed his company for nine years, after he'd walked in our front door as a kitten. We had named him Jeffrey after a poem by Christopher Smart.

All our charity tins were stolen one night in December, which was annoying. But we were amused because they also stole two purses full of foreign coins. When they discovered that, they scattered the coins all over the front path.

Soon it was time for the usual family Christmas with Sue and Miles, which we all enjoy so much. I decided it was time for us to give a New Year's Eve party, so we did - for about twenty family and friends, but just for lunch and a few silly games, not forgetting 'Auld Lang Syne', which we had to sing in the garden.

Now I must find my 1992 diary and see what happened then!

1992

At first glance it seems to have been a very busy year for us both, so I shall enjoy going over it with you. At the start of 1992, I note from my diary that I bravely tackled a Women's Institute on the Mainland at Lymington. I talked about my war-time experiences with the GAR. I enjoyed this, and it was for their birthday celebrations.

On 16th January 1992 I say in my diary that a whole load of heavy surrealist books fell on top of David in the middle of the night. This was quite a crisis, but neither of us was badly hurt. As we weren't travelling off anyway, I managed to do a lot more French teaching. It is encouraging that all my adult pupils have been faithfully coming since 1981! A special pleasure was given me when Jean Harrison took her GCSE in 1998 and obtained an 'A' pass. When she started she didn't know a word of French, but her exceptional dedication and cheerfulness made her an ideal pupil. I treasure the friendship I have with all my pupils, and it has improved my French too. How I wish I could make use of it in France, but I fear our travelling days are over now.

Most of January was taken up with the planning of my seventieth birthday party. This was to take place on 1st February at the George Hotel, Yarmouth, with seventy guests to celebrate with me. I share my birthday with two dear friends, Christine Colt-Williams and Jade Fletcher, so they came to enjoy it with me. Jade was only nine then, and from a family that we had shared out lives with since 1966. Chrissy has been a close friend since then too. Anyway, it was a wonderful party. David Clarke of the George prepared a beautiful feast for us all. My son Kevin made a charming speech. All the family came and, at the end, we all sang. There was no room for dancing. I was most grateful to my dear friend Liz Sydenham for driving a car-load of us in thick fog from Cowes to Yarmouth. It was indeed an act of true friendship because she knew I wanted to have a drink or two at the party. Also our dear friends the Marshes drove from London, bringing a friend of David's called Bettina Shaw-Lawrence. It was a party to be remembered for ever. It's a good age to celebrate, before getting too old, and yet young enough to enjoy it.

I had two cakes at the party, one made by my dear friend Kath Barnes, who has made all the family birthday cakes over the past forty years, and Liz made a surprise one with a frog on it. All in all I was 'spoilt rotten', and enjoyed every minute of it. Towards the end of February 1992, we went to stay with my brother Ben and Joan. They are such perfect hosts, and they made a fuss of us. Ben always arranges for me to meet up with all my Marlow friends. This time was special for me because he took me up to see our farm cottage where Michael and I spent the first few years of our marriage.

Home again for a few weeks before David's operation for a hernia and prostate trouble. This wasn't as awful as we expected, and he was home after only a week. In early April we were off to Birmingham for a Quaker Conference. David had to speak on 'The Inadequacy of Words'. The Conference took place in one of the large Bourneville-Cadbury houses where we all stayed for three nights. Adrian Cairns was our host and organiser. I enjoyed the silent seances of the Quakers.

It was so much better than the false conversation which happens when strangers meet. Adrian had gathered some distinguished speakers — Bishop Peter Firth, (one of my favourites on *Thought for the Day*). He spoke well and read some of R S Thomas' poetry. Jane Lapotaire, the actress, was fascinating when she told us the story of her life. Unity Spencer, daughter of the great Stanley Spencer, spoke about the 'Confrontation of Art'. David had a full house for his talk on the 'Inadequacy of Words', and it was much appreciated.

One evening, David and I had to go to the house of Peter Zackis to give a poetry reading. We were very squashed up in his sitting room, but he was most grateful to David for going. It meant that we missed the last night concert where most of us were asked to perform. On the way home we stayed at Jenny's converted pub in Jericho in Oxford. Emma, my granddaughter, was there too so we had a wonderful welcome and supper in a nearby restaurant. Jenny was off the next day at 7 am and she had given us her big double bed for a good night's sleep. We then decided to call on Sophie and Robin Waterfield. They gave us lunch and it was good to be with them again. They are both special and Robin does so much for depressed friends. We still keep in touch and he sends regular uplifting letters. We had a very wet journey back to the Island. April 9th 1992 was another Election Day, and boringly the Tories were in, but with a smaller majority. I'm sad that politics doesn't interest me as much as it did! At least we don't have the horrors of the Thatcher regime.

In April 1992 I became a guinea-pig for Patricia Veck. This meant two hours of blissful aromatherapy in the shape of a full massage. I had six of these half-price treatments, and now I go every fortnight and it is the best thing in the world. I used to tell myself that when I became rich enough I would be regularly massaged, so that is yet another ambition fulfilled!

Easter was in mid-April in 1992. It's a celebration that I love! I am always asked to read David's *Ecce Homo* in church on Good Friday, and I'm glad to do that. Also that year I was invited to do the narration of 'Jerusalem Joy', ably produced by Tressa Lambert and her choir. We did this in two churches, and I really enjoyed it. Apart from that we had the ritual Easter Monday egg hunt in the garden.

We had a very warm May, so I indulged myself all day in the garden. When my face became swollen and red, I felt quite ill and I took myself off to the doctor. He declared that it was something called 'rosacea', a kind of virus which is also aggravated by red wine! I had to take antibiotics and drive David off to Manchester for his next date at the French Department of the University. We decided to go via Chorley and visit out old friend and poet Phoebe Hesketh. Now in her mid eighties, she is still as beautiful as ever. I met her first in the early sixties at Denman College, when we both attended Miss Bird's course on Public Speaking. We have been firm friends ever since, and she much approved of my marriage to David. However, after a good supper we had to find our way to her home-help's house. On the way there I stopped to ask the way at a garage, and walked into a glass door, so I arrived quite tearfully and with a black eye.

The night accommodation wasn't much fun because in order to get to the loo, which usually happens three or four times a night, I had to pass two alsatians who snarled at me, but after a quick breakfast we found our way to a pleasant hotel which had been booked for us, and so on to the French Seminar. This was an all day session, all in French and geared up to the 'African French' poets. David became very lucid with his French comments, and we had a very amusing supper with all the French people. David's talk was on Saturday and it was all fairly laid back with a really good finishing party at Ken Brown's house which went on very late.

My rosacea was a nuisance, but I flirted shamelessly with a French professor who said my accent was delicious! We drove home during a Bank Holiday heatwave and caught quite an early boat at 4 pm.

My face was really painful by then, so I went off to see the doctor again and he prescribed some soothing treatment. David was busy writing a review of Kathleen Raine's poetry for Resurgence. My face affliction went on being painful for two weeks. I hated not being able to be in the sun. Giving a talk to the wives of the Lions was quite an ordeal. It was called 'Is life worth Living?' I felt a bit sick trying to eat the huge dinner at the York Hotel in Ryde, and almost felt that it wasn't!

In June 1992 David and I were off to a reception at Quay Arts, in Newport, to do with a Tennyson anniversary. We took our Romanian friend Christina (who was researching Benjamin Fondane) to meet the Romanian Ambassador who was our host on the Island. David worked hard on Bill Hayter's obituary. We gave a reading together at Tennyson's Library at the Farringford Hotel. Sue won the Rose Bowl for her golf, and I felt very proud.

On 29th June 1992 we were off to Avignon for Larry Durrell's seminar arranged by the MacNivens. Jean-Claude Masson met us at Charles de Gaulle Airport and we all lunched together at the huge Gare de Lyons before catching the efficient T.V. to Avignon. We were nearly late for the reception supper, but all was well and we were welcomed and given the plans for the week. It was very hot but we had a cool basement hotel room. After our usual lazy breakfast in bed we taxied to the very grand Palais des Papes to meet all the other guests. Susan and Ian MacNiven introduced us to everyone, and there was a great atmosphere. The opening speeches were all paying tribute to Larry Durrell. We lunched outside the Palais des Papes in the warm sunshine. I went back to our hotel for a snooze because I wanted to be ready for the Town Hall reception, where we were all given kir to drink and my favourite; kir royale, cassis with champagne! When that was over five of us walked to the *Encre de Tacke* with Liz who is studying Elizabeth Smart. We were invited to a conference in Ottawa next June, but I don't suppose we will be able to make that. The next day it was David's turn to talk about Lawrence Durrell. He was given the usual adulation and Ian MacNiven paid him 1,000 francs as an honorarium. The evening ended with another *al fresco* dinner, and riding on the Carousel. F J Temple and I were really delighted by it! The conference next day had some distinguished speakers: Jacques Carriere and Larry Gamache on Gnostics. Liz talking about Elizabeth Smart and Anäis Nin, with David adding an amusing anecdote. Later he joined the panel for a poetry and writing discussions.

We enjoyed the farewell dinner party, but we had a problem the next day because of the French trucker's strike. They had not only blocked all the main roads out of Avignon, but had strewn all their vegetables and fruit all over the town. We had been invited to stay with Anne Minkowski, about forty miles away. No buses were working because of the strike, so we decided to take a taxi. This worked quite well and we passed by the Marquis de Sade's estate!

It was peaceful staying with Anne. She took us to Gordes and Roussillons. Patrick Hutchinson came to spend the day with his beautiful Nikki and her son.

I spent most of the time in the pool. There was a violent thunderstorm the night before we left. Anne drove us to catch the TGV in Avignon, which was crowded with French school-children. François Xavier Jaujard met us at the Gare de Lyons and drove us all the way to the Airport. He was so kind and generous and we mourn his recent death. The 'plane was very late, but we managed to catch a ferry and Bernard Pratt, our Liberal president, gave us a lift home.

The next excitement was finding a suitable dress for the Buckingham Palace Garden Party. I found quite a nice navy-blue and white-striped dress at our Church Bazaar. David decided to wear his Simpson suit, so off we went to stay the night at Marion's near the Barbican. She was away but had lent us the key.

We had our photos taken outside the Palace. (I wasn't keen on my new hat!). As we were queuing up we met David's great poet friend, Michael Hamburger and his wife, Anne, so we spent all the time at the party with them. David was delighted and they might have been sitting in our back garden for all the notice they took of all the grand people and the gardens. Anne and I struggled to get the food to their table. It was all very different from when we went in 1976, and it was a question of 'Oh, help yourself!' (This is a family joke too long to explain).

It drizzled quite a lot, but we were under the big trees. Anne and I did a bit of 'famous-people spotting', and we were quite near the Royal Marquee. We were glad to leave early, and to be escorted to a taxi by a policeman. That night David took me to a very special dinner. Afterwards Alistair Brotchie, of Atlas Press, one of David's publishers, joined us back at Marion's flat for a really good talk about everything.

Simon Callow had arranged for us to see his production of *Shades* the next day. I say in my diary 'This wasn't a very good play, but Simon's exuberance and charm, and a good supper made it a memorable evening'.

We made the most of being in London and went to the Manet exhibition at the new part of the National Gallery. In the evening we dined with Jeremy Trafford and Adam Johnson. It was a merry party, with beautifully-cooked food by the poet Adam. It is so sad that such a brilliant poet should now be dead from that wretched AIDS.

Another drama overtook us on our drive home in the Nissan. We had stopped for lunch with Mel Gooding, at Castlenau, where I should have filled the car up with water. On the M3 Motorway we reached boiling point and the whole car shuddered to a halt. No AA telephones had been installed on the new stretch of Motorway, so we were really stuck. However, I bravely climbed down the very steep slope across a field, and into a nearby house who's owner let me use a telephone for the AA. This all took nearly an hour, so I hurried back to the car only to find David had fallen asleep. At last a very patronising AA man arrived who treated us as is we were a couple of old 'dements'. By that time David had woken up and demanded that we be taken to a 'Tea House' as he put it. This confirmed the AA man's suspicions that we were quite potty! However, he agreed to tow us to a Country Park which was en route to Portsmouth. We invited him to enjoy tea with us, which he declared was 'against the rules', but he gave in and when he overheard that we'd been to Buckingham Palace, he became more affable. Finally, he agreed to tow us to Portsmouth Car Ferry. He also made arrangements for us to be met by another AA towing car at Fishbourne on the Island. There was a hairy moment when the Wightlink Ferry said they wouldn't take the car unless we could drive it on. By some miracle the car started and we limped on. We were met by another dubious AA man, who said it would ruin the car if he had to tow it to Cowes, so we told him we didn't care. We were thankfully home by 9 pm. The next day I was told the Nissan needed a whole new engine, and that I'd be without a car for a week. I was so pleased we had survived the breakdown I hardly blinked when the bill came to £900.

At the beginning of August 1992 a television crew came to stay. They camped in the garden and filmed David all day. Chris Foster, an artist, interviewed David with a cameraman and a sound man. When night fell, they persuaded David to read some of his *Night Thoughts* in the floodlit garden. On Sunday afternoon they interviewed me on camera, but I had to do it twice because there was no film in it the first time, so it wasn't very spontaneous. Later we heard that they were very pleased with the results, and were hoping to sell it to a Television Company, but now seven years on it hasn't happened so I never get very excited about these enterprises.

On 9th August 1992 we were off for a Poetry Festival at Escorial near Madrid. We taxied all the way to Heathrow and were escorted to the 1st Class lounge before the flight. This is how I like to do it! A waiting car drove us from Madrid to the Hotel Euroform which was in a beautiful position overlooking King Philip's castle. We were met by Tom Doyle the organiser. Soon Kathleen Richmond and Keith Pritchard arrived for drinks with us. They both teach at Sandown High School and, although they had arranged to meet us there, I didn't think it would really happen. Meals are late in Spain, so it was almost 10 pm before we joined up with the Syrian poet Adonis, and Georgio from Budapest, and Lasse from Sweden for a welcome dinner with plenty of good Spanish wine.

Our bedroom was cool with a beautiful view. We went down for breakfast to hear about the day's plans.

An old Spanish lady of ninety-two was invited to open the conference, which she did with great charm, and a professor talked for about two hours. Then Adonis read his poetry to us. The rest of the day was spent celebrating Tom Doyle's birthday, so I only have a hazy memory of it.

The following day Alexander Petrov, who is half Russian and half Yugoslavian, read his new poem 'The Prado in Flames' which was very dramatic. We spent the whole day with him and his wife, Crinka, who wanted to interview David for Yugoslavian Television.

Jeanine and Lasse took me to an excellent classical concert in an old theatre at 11 pm. As we were on show in the front row, Lasse kept nudging me to keep awake. David didn't come because he wanted to prepare his readings for the next day.

This went very well, and John Liddy, the Irish Poet, read with him. Jeanine, the Spanish actress, also read all David's poems in Spanish, most beautifully.

On the last day we went with the American poet, Louis Bourne, and John Liddy to the Escorial Castle and Museum. It was vast with some good El Greco paintings.

Late that evening Clara, the Spanish organiser, took us with Jeanine for supper *al fresco* in the village, and that brought our Spanish visit to a close. It had been generously paid for by the Spanish Government. We were all given presents on our departure.

We left Madrid Airport with a German poet and his wife for an uneventful journey home for a change.

Marion, Alison and Jade had looked after the house while we were away, so it was good to find it all spick and span and full of flowers on our return. We had a letter from Chris Foster, who had organised the television programme in our house, saying we would get £2,000 when it was televised, but so far nothing had happened!

At the end of August Jake had a Ceilidh to celebrate his eighteenth birthday. We all danced to an Irish Folk Band, and I think it was the very last time I was able to dance before the arthritis really took over.

Also, to celebrate the August Bank Holiday, David and I bought a summer-house from Corrals. It was a special offer for £500, including the erection of it. It was really for David to write in, but that didn't come off. May christened it 'Toad Hall', and its been quite a boon ever since. I moved a spare bed into it, so that friends could sleep there in the summer. Over the last seven years we've had a great many sleeping there. I like to rest in it in the afternoons.

In September 1992 we were off to London again at the invitation of Channel 4 News, who were making a film called *The Art of Tripping*.

This took place in an old warehouse near London Bridge. A limo came to fetch us from Marion's, and we were taken to the Green Room to talk to George Melly who was also waiting. We were given hospitality, and I much enjoyed talking to Bernard Hill, who is one of my favourite actors, and narrating the whole programme. After David was made up, we went into a huge warehouse where the Director was shouting at everyone. Finally, David was interviewed and asked to read a poem. We were sent off in a taxi, with our supper packed up, with £50, and they had booked us into the best seats to see a French film that David fancied, called *Les Amants du Pont Neuf,* which suited us very well. Months later we watched the result on Channel 4 Television. It was mostly about the results of drug-taking. While we were in London we took the opportunity of spending an evening with Stephen and Natasha Spender, and dining with Christine Wild.

I had my Visa card and cheque-book stolen in London, when I carelessly left them in a Lloyds Bank. My signature was forged and £100 drawn every day on my account. Luckily Lloyds Bank put a stop to it and charged me nothing. I'll try not to be so careless again.

In October Jane Dunn came to stay because she wanted to ask David about his relationship with Antonia White. The biography she produced became a best-seller in 1998. The last two months of 1992 went by quite swiftly, and we didn't go off again.

1993

When I'm writing about all David's invitations abroad, I get worried that I won't record them properly, but 1993 was the start of us going more slowly. Mostly people came to stay with us. We still had a spare bedroom then.

David had several examinations at St Mary's Hospital in the early part of the year, but nothing special was revealed in spite of his bladder and tummy pains. It also meant that he didn't feel like writing much.

Kevin went off on a truck-driving trip to Russia with a friend, and had quite a hairy time. I was glad when he returned safely.

We celebrated our 18th wedding anniversary with Alan Clodd, and I gave a dinner party on May 17th with June and Neville Braybrooke.

We heard, very sadly, that Adam Johnson the poet, died around that time.

In June 1993, Stephen Stuart-Smith, David's new Enitharmon publisher, arrived with champagne, so we had an hilarious lunch. Marion helped me. David signed all the Oscar Vladislas de Lubicz Milosz translations, which Stephen has made into such a nice publication. He left for London with Marion in the evening. He is so devoted to David, and prepared to do so much for him. Alan Clodd has found a marvellous person to carry on with his Enitharmon publications.

I went back to teaching the Swedish students again. Quite a small party with Sven, their leader. They took to acting my version of *Macbeth* with alacrity. I was amazed by the way they handled the Shakespearean language. I had two classes, the very clever ones and the not-so-clever. The latter tackled *A Midsummer Night's Dream* very well indeed. On the last week we gave performances to each other. Sven was very impressed. It was a very easy time for me, and I was extremely well paid. Kevin took us in his coach to various places.

In July of 1993, Jenny invited me to a concert at Taplow Court, the headquarters of the Buddhists. There was a special concert there, and one of the guests wanted to recite extracts from David's *Night Thoughts*. Of course I wanted to be there. Sue fetched me and drove us very efficiently to Marlow to stay with Ben and Joan. I felt a bit anxious at leaving David all on his own, but I had arranged for a friend to take him shopping, and it was only for two nights.

We enjoyed the visit very much. Edward and Pippy asked us over to their large house and garden. I also showed Sue the house where she was born, and the new owners let us look into the actual bedroom.

The concert at Taplow Court was very moving too. I gave the young man who had worked so well on David's *Night Thoughts,* a copy of David's *Collected Poems,* and he was very grateful. I am very pleased that Jenny is a Buddhist: it has made such a difference to her life and my grand-daughter, Emma, is also a Buddhist. I don't find it aggravates my Christian belief at all.

On our last Sunday in Marlow, Ben had arranged for my great friend, Rachel White, and his daughter, Katy, who is very special and an excellent school-teacher (I like to think its in the blood), to call for a chat.

We left Marlow after Sunday lunch and were home for tea. David and our cat Jason gave us a great welcome.

Also in July I was presented with a framed certificate thanking me for twenty-years devoted service to Hospital broadcasting. I was really pleased to have that. Charles and I put on a special poetry programme that night, to celebrate.

Still in July I dragged David to have a consultation with a Mr Hoare, a homeopathic doctor. He gave us lots of advice, but I didn't really take to him. We only had four visits to him.

I had my usual party in Milo's woods for all my pupils, and a scavenger hunt. Rhiane from New Zealand called for the weekend. She is working for Stephen Stuart-Smith, and she was rather shy of David so I took her for a swim at Gurnard Bay.

In August, Ramona Fotiade from Romania came to stay. She was researching a writer-philospher called Benjamin Fondane; whom David knew well in the late 1930s. We became very attached to her and her husband who works for the BBC's World Service. On August Bank Holiday I attended the Cheshire Home Fête. I had been to twenty-two of them non-stop. Now, alas, it is too difficult to manage a stall, and I miss them.

In November a lorry crashed into my Nissan, which was a nasty shock, but I wasn't hurt. It happened very near Northwood Garage, so I was persuaded to buy an automatic Ford Fiesta. It cost £4,000 but its been a real boon ever since. I would be marooned now without a car.

Also, our new kitten Thomas, arrived to live with us. He was only three weeks old, but now nearing six years old, he has become quite a treasured cat in spite of his wicked ways. He's given nearly all of us quite bad bites. Recently he has emerged from that ordeal to become much more tolerant.

I note in my 1993 diary that I had quite a treat on October 30th. A book of tributes to Bob Dylan was to be launched at the Troubadour in London. All contributors were invited to the party. I had written briefly about my role as his housekeeper on the Isle of Wight. We were all invited to read our pieces. Kevin drove me up and came to the party. There was a great gathering of all Dylan's fans, and they were eager to know what he had been like as a house-guest! The Isle of Wight County Press featured me holding the Bob Dylan book, and recounting my time as a housekeeper for him in 1969!

For Christmas 1993, Sarah Wilson came for dinner with a Serbian called Alex. He was fasting so he didn't appreciate all the good food I'd laid on for them. They stayed at a nearby hotel.

For the first time ever I left David alone on Christmas Day, and went with eighty-nine-year-old May for the Christmas lunch with Sue, Miles and family. David seemed really pleased to have the day to himself. He hasn't been feeling very well for ages. I left him on Boxing Day too for the hockey match, taking my neighbour, Gareth Beaumont, to join in the fun and the Trivial Pursuit afterwards.

Then I had to prepare for the visit of Michael Wishart. He came with one of his beautiful paintings for us, but he only stayed for one night and that was the end of 1993. Not a good one for David healthwise.

1993

1994

In January 1994 we had a visit from the BBC. The Programme was called *Poets under Fire!* Judith Bumpus and Valentine Cunningham arrived to spend the evening with us to record David for Radio 3. It was a programme to do with the Spanish Civil War and 1930s poetry. It sounded quite good when we heard it a few weeks later. They came with two bottles of good white wine, so I gave them fish for dinner.

Also in January, Alan Clodd came to stay with us. He helped out with all David's papers and letters. I was worried when he complained of a pain in his chest, so he agreed to come to the Medical Clinic. Dr Bol insisted that he went into hospital and there he stayed, having lots of heart tests for four days. Eventually, he was well enough to return to his home in London. We were worried for him, especially as he is nearly eighty and also has diabetes, but I believe that he is quite sensible about that. Poor David had to go to St Mary's again for a painful bladder check-up. I fear this is becoming a medical history book.

Alan returned to London, looking frail but swearing he was out of pain. I had a quiet seventy-second birthday party at the Horse & Groom Inn with most of my family.

In February, thanks to Gavin Ewart, David was reinstated as a Fellow of the Royal Society of Literature, but we didn't feel like going up for that celebration later in the year.

The highlight of the month was the visit of Roger Scott from Newcastle. He had written quite a few 'fan' letters to David, which I had answered, and I was longing to meet him. I wasn't disappointed because he was totally charming in every way. I put in my diary of February 15th 1994 when I met him off the ferry at Ryde Pier, 'Roger is tall, slim, very out-going, and intelligent'. He and David talked all evening and I'm sure he helped David forget all his medical pains. Sadly Roger had to return to Newcastle the next day. Again to quote my diary, I say: 'Its been such a good visit, and because of David I have found a really good friend'. These words were most prophetic because no-one has helped David more over the last five years.

The next day the most beautiful bouquet of Interflora jasmine arrived as a thank-you from Roger. Could one ask for more?

The weather was horrible that February, with sleety snow every day. At the end of the month David had to go to St Mary's Hospital for more tests and X-rays, which was a worry.

In March David had the whole of his *Night Thoughts* read by
James Roose-Evans at a Temenos concert in London. It was well received, and
they sent us a tape of it.

Also in February my Jenny came for a nice long weekend. She slipped all the
way downstairs, but luckily didn't hurt herself very much.

On 1st March 1994 we had to go to St Mary's for the result of David's X-Rays.
Happily they were good, and no horrid cancer growth had shown up. So David
cheered up a little.

In March we had the bad news that the roof needed re-doing. That cost us
over £4,000. Also the hole in the spare bedroom ceiling had to be repaired and
decorated, so that was another £1,000, but it was all essential work!

Peter Lambert taught me how to give out the wine at the Communion services.
I felt very privileged to do this for three years, before my stupid arthritis made
it impossible.

Author Ian Gibson, a charming Irishman, came to stay at the end of March. He
lives in Spain and has written in great detail about Salvador Dalí. He wanted to
ask David about when he had stayed with Dalí for a week in Paris in 1935. I
say in my diary, 'Ian had been like a flash of warm sunlight in our lives!'

My brother Ben had a fairly serious operation in 1994, but he came through it
so well, and made no fuss about it. In April all South Africans were allowed to
vote, and we shared in their joy on the television.

On 30th May 1994, Sue had one of her riotous family parties. We had a funny
frog game; you had to toss it in the air and try to catch it in a cup. We all had a
go, and I ran backwards and fell into a flower bed breaking my wrist. The
family were so sympathetic but insisted that I went to Casualty. I quite enjoyed
all the fuss they made of me, and after an X-Ray, I was plastered up. Sue drove
me home and David was most concerned. Apart from not being able to write
very well, or drive a car for six weeks, I did everything as normal. The really
sad thing that happened on 30th May 1994 was that my dear friend June
Braybrooke died in London. Neville rang that night to tell us. It was his
birthday and he was being so brave about it. I'm so glad that we see him
regularly now with his step-daughter, Victoria, who came down to Cowes to
set up home with him. Two very precious people.

The family were so sympathetic over my accident; Jenny stayed on to help and
Milo sent Interflora flowers from America where he was touring with Elvis
Costello.

On 6th June 1994 we had lots of media coverage for the fiftieth anniversary of
D-Day. It was good to be able to be really lazy, but the house was so untidy

and dirty. There were very touching obituaries about June in all the papers, which I've kept. Towards the end of the month I used to wiggle off my plaster so that I could write properly, but I had to wait until the end of June before the plaster came off officially and I could then drive again. I don't think this is of much interest to anyone but myself!

Also, in June 1994 something happened to make us quite newsworthy. Christine Wild had told the editor of Independent Review that she thought we would make ideal subjects for a series they were running, called *How we Met.* They agreed, and Jenny Gilbert came down for lunch to interview us separately about it. Then George Wright, a journalist photographer, came a week later to take colour photos of us in 'Toad Hall'. The result was quite a spread on 31st July 1994 so, of course, I was a bit thrilled and had quite a few photocopies done. It briefly told the story of our lives since meeting in 1974. A documentary lady from the BBC kept ringing about doing a programme about us, but I was quite content with the Independent article, and I'm glad to have a concise, journalistic account of how we did meet. The same day as we were photographed, Sue rang me to say Emma was engaged to Paul Morgan, so it was a very happy time for us all.

Alan Clodd came to stay again. They were preparing to republish David's Translations of French Poets, so he wanted David to answer lots of questions about them.

In July, I was very flattered because Anne Toms asked if I would be one of the speakers at the Quay Arts Centre, at the setting up of the Steve Ross Memorial Trust. This happened on 16th July 1994. Brenda was there with all her children. There were many tributes to Steve by auspicious people. Mine was quite low key, and called 'These Foolish Things remind me of Steve'. James Nye played it beautifully on the piano. I was given a bouquet, followed by a concert, so it was quite an occasion. On July 15th we celebrated Mary's birthday with lunch in the garden. She provided everything as usual and we had a good laugh. This has become quite a ritual. On 28th July, Ian Gibson arrived with a television crew to interview David in the garden about the time he spent with Salvador Dalí in Paris. This was a real fun-day because they all brought plenty of wine and we lunched in the garden. The interview went with a swing. When we watched it on the television a few months later, we were really pleased with the result.

In August we had lots of visitors to stay. Liz Podnieks and her fiancé from Toronto. She wanted to pick David's brains about Elizabeth Smart. Then the next week we had three young publishers from Sweden. We had met them in Malmö in the 1980s and they wanted to see the Isle of Wight. All three had to sleep together in our spare room, but they were appreciative and enjoyed watching the birds in Newtown Creek.

We had met all of them at the Malmö Festival, and they had published a
bi-lingual edition of David's poetry. Finally, in August, Denis Egan and his
partner Stéphane came for a long weekend. We had met Denis some time ago
in Paris, and he wanted to do David's biography. He is American with
bi-lingual French, and works for a big publishing company in Paris. Annie
Goosens came to meet them, and Denis taped her conversation about the old
days when she and David were very young. Kathleen Raine was on television
after being given the Queen's Gold Medal for poetry, and we enjoyed watching
her interview.

I've been re-reading my diary for the end of 1994. We had the usual big quota
of visitors, and I had more pupils than ever. The Prayer Group met here; the
WI wasn't too bad, and Charles and I read poetry on Hospital Radio every two
weeks. Stephen Stuart-Smith paid a lunch-time visit for David to sign his
Selected Poems. He made it, as always, a festive occasion with plenty of
champagne.

On Tuesday 6th December 1994 we had some bad luck. I returned rather late
from Hospital Radio, and I was dismayed to find David lying in the dark on the
dining-room floor. He had fallen while trying to put his supper tray onto the
table. He was very cold, distressed and in pain. I covered him over with a
blanket and dialled 999. The ambulance men managed quite well, and I
followed to St Mary's in my car. We had quite a long wait in the emergency
ward, but they managed an X-Ray on the trolley. As it looked quite serious,
they admitted David to Luccombe Ward, and I came home feeling very lost and
worried.

I went to see David the next day at noon. He complained that waiting for an
operation whilst on a trolley was 'like being at Hyde Park Corner' with all the
trolleys queuing up and knocking into each other. The nurses were amused at
this remark!

He came through the ordeal fairly well, and when I saw him on the evening
after his operation, I was able to help him with his supper. One leg had to be
in traction all the time, so he wasn't very comfortable. After a few days, I
realised that David wouldn't be home for Christmas, so I was resigned to that.
I went every day to visit, and so did our friends. At first David wasn't too bad
in Hospital because over Christmas they really make an effort to decorate the
wards and to be jolly. Charles and I used to dedicate our Hospital Radio
poems to David, but he wasn't able to hear it very well. I tried to make the best
of being alone for Christmas, and it passed quite quickly.

There was so much to do with the usual parties, and May Shenton's ninetieth
birthday to organize. I don't think I neglected David because so many friends
went to visit, and I called every day. But after the excitement of Christmas,

David became more and more depressed. He wasn't even interested when Seán Street arranged a Radio Retrospective about him. He and Julian May came down on 20th January 1995 to record an interview with me. The resulting programme called *A Burning Sound,* about David's life and work, and included interviews with Christine Jordis in Paris, Philip Marsh, Kathleen Raine and Jeremy Reed. It was a great success and I'm glad we have plenty of tapes of it. Alan Clodd came to stay to hear the broadcast on 28th January, and we had many telephone calls of congratulations afterwards. I had been asked to read 'September Sun' by David, the poem which had brought us together in 1973, and that was quite a thrill for me to hear myself on a BBC programme.

Whilst visiting David, a bit late, I stabbed my leg on a tree support in the car park. When I arrived by his bed with a bleeding shin, I burst into tears. A kindly nurse sent me in a wheelchair to Casualty, where I was given much sympathy, some stitches, and an anti-Tetanus injection. I was told to take no baths and call to have it redressed every day. In a strange way, I think it was a call for help, and I rather enjoyed the pampering; it fitted in well with the visit anyway.

1994

1995

On 1st January 1995 I took David some whisky and vodka on the advice of Dr Michael Laurence and Parvin. I hope he's allowed to have it. Also, Simon Callow 'phoned from Japan in order to give David words of comfort and cheer.

My great friend, Brenda Ross, celebrated her seventieth birthday in January 1995. She persuaded me to be driven down in my car by her son Hugh Ross with Maggie to make up the foursome. It made a wonderful break, and we had big celebrations at Herb Cottage and a nearby Village Hall.

Upon my return, on a bitterly cold night, I was told that three prisoners had escaped from the Albany Prison, and were in the Northwood District. After visiting David in Luccombe Ward, I had to return to our empty dark house. I was a bit afraid that the prisoners might be squatting there, but I have extremely kind neighbours who saw me safely indoors. It was also helpful to know that my neighbour, Mr Beaumont, is an Officer at Camp Hill Prison. My leg took three weeks to heal, and I really appreciated the first bath I had then.

On 1st February 1995, it was completely unexpected when Sue arranged a surprise party. Kevin called me and said he would drive me to Sue's house to collect a birthday plant. When I entered the sitting room there was a collection of all my nearest and dearest friends, including Jenny from Oxford and Kath with a cake. Sue had chosen twelve friends with such care, and I was really thrilled to have such a party. I just didn't believe that anyone could fool me so easily! We had a sit-down lunch and they all clapped me to my seat! Later I was driven to see David, who was quite himself. He had arranged Interflora flowers for me too.

That evening I had a party here with all my French pupils, which had been pre-arranged, so it was a birthday to remember.

Early in February David was moved to Rookwood Ward in St Mary's Hospital. It's for the very old and disabled. Although it was easier to get to, I was sad to watch David getting more and more inert and depressed. Even a very good full-page article about him in the Independent on Sunday didn't cheer him. Denis Egan had written it, and it was full of praise. When I wasn't able to get much information about David's return home from the nurses, I had a meeting with a Dr Patell who wasn't really helpful, and he ordered David to have a brain scan. I gathered later that this was a horrid ordeal. I don't want to dwell too long on the first difficult months of 1995. I finally decided to get a stairlift installed, and work for David's release. Finally on 17th March David was returned in an ambulance. Before that, I had several helpful visits from the Social Services giving advice on how to cope. Poor David had painful bed-sores, so the District nurse came every day as well as carers. I was so pleased to have him home, I felt I could cope with anything. Ray, the local male District Nurse, was so helpful and he cheered up both of us. I owe him quite a debt. Also, our carer Sue, came cheerfully every day to cope and also a 'tucker up'. Gradually things improved and by the end of the summer David came down in the stair-lift for meals. For the month of September, he was full of writing ideas and on a real high. I had some thank-you tea-parties for all who had helped. A special person was Mrs Bell, a top physiotherapist at St Mary's, who had firmly insisted that David walked again! His accident completely changed our way of life, and apart from one or two mishaps, we weren't really too bad. We had a pressing 'phone call from Mike Goldmark in Uppingham, who wanted to hire the Albert Hall in October and to put on his favourite poets. As David was unable to get there the writer, Ian Sinclair, came down with a film crew so that David could appear on a screen at the Albert Hall concert. It was fun having them for the day. Ian Sinclair even wrote a poem about it, which he read on National Poetry Day at the new theatre at the Quay Arts. Roger Scott came to visit us again. We like him more each time, and he stayed with Liz at the Flower Pot.

A new friend came into our lives in August 1995, Matt Kittay, a teacher of comparative religion at Sandown High School. He wrote such a nice letter that I couldn't resist asking him over for tea. He comes to see us regularly and he is such an 'encourager'. A most delightful friend to have and he supports us with everything.

Alan Clodd came down too, and he was most helpful to me when David was going through rather a difficult stage. Since trying to write these memoirs, I have come to realise what a really frustrating time writers must have, and I admire them so much. I feel guilty about the many times when I thought David should be working more regularly at his writing.

Towards the end of 1995 I made another good friend. It was Len Townsend, he had recently become blind and needed a lift to church when his wife of over fifty years of marriage became too crippled to take him. He is now aged ninety-one, and one of my best friends and advisors. He was so brave when his wife had to be in St Mary's after a fall. He went every day to see her, and I used to take him on Sundays. Even when things were at their worst, he always managed to cheer us all up with his wry sense of humour. Very sadly, his wife, Kit, died in hospital in July 1996. I was proud to read a poem dedicated to her at the funeral service. We arranged a good lunch party for Len's ninetieth birthday at the Bowsprit: all his church friends came and he paid for the whole thing most generously. Now that Len is in St Vincent's of Ryde, he goes to the nearby church and sometimes comes to our church at Northwood. I treasure his friendship and we have quite long telephone talks.

On July 8th 1995, my granddaughter Emma married Paul Morgan. This was a very happy day for all of us. Sue and Miles had arranged for a huge marquee to be put up in their garden, and over one hundred of us had a sit-down meal. But it started earlier in Newport at the Registry Office for a select few of us. Emma's bridesmaids were Poppy and Rosie, aged twelve and eight, and they looked so enchanting. We have some beautiful photographs of them all. After the civil ceremony we all met at Holmfield for the Buddhist Blessing, well organized by my Jenny and her Oxford friends. It was very moving and we have it on video. Then came the great meal, followed by some really amusing speeches. Kevin and Miles both excelled in this. Finally we all danced in the marquee and in the field. There was a really happy family atmosphere. I can't name all the guests, but it was lovely for me to see Valerie and Ian Francis at my table, from the old Stratford-upon-Avon days. The next day Christie Wild and Annie Goosens came to us for lunch. The weather was perfect too.

Emma and Paul went to Crete for their honeymoon. I love all my grandchildren, but Emma has a very special place in my heart because I looked after her a lot of the time for the first two years of her life. She is now about to be thirty, and a most caring granddaughter. Alan Clodd came for the wedding weekend to look after David, because he was still unable to do much for himself. Another very dear granddaughter called Zoe range to say that she was engaged to a traffic-controller called Peter Lee, and they would marry in February 1996, so I was pleased to think there was another wedding coming soon. In August 1995, Zoe brought Peter for tea and we liked him very much. David wrote a poem called *Ivy* which the Independent published on his seventy-ninth birthday, and later it was included in his Selected Poems published by Emitharmon in 1995.

While David was still in hospital early in 1995, he had a letter from the French Embassy saying they would like to make him a Chevalier dans i'Ordre National des Arts et Lettres. This cheered him up a little, but it wasn't until June 1996 before he was well enough to receive the medal at the French Institute in London. This took a lot of arranging on my part, and I'll write about it later when I get into the year of 1996! David had a page of a diary he's written recently published in the London Review of Books. Then he told me that he thought we should collaborate with my old diaries so that he could write a 2,000 word article for them. I was pleased he thought it a good idea, but nothing came of it in the end. At the end of 1995, Karl Orend of Alyscamps Press produced a neat little book of David's *Night Thoughts*. It had a Lucien Freud portrait of David on the cover, and it also contained Simon Callow's thoughts on meeting David and an appreciation of David's work by Kathleen Raine. Karl also wrote an afterword, and dedicated the book to me, which was quite a thrill. Neville wrote a fulsome review of it for the Tablet. It is so sad that now in 1999 the Alyscamps Press in Paris has come to an end.

Also in September 1995 I note that the poet, Jenny Joseph, came for supper after she had given a reading at St Mary's. A charming person and a good poet.

Charles decided it was time to retire from Hospital Radio and I think he was wise, but I miss the regular readings of poetry and I have no tapes to give Len anymore. Roger Scott came to visit us again in September 1995, (Liz joined us for supper and then she took him back for B&B at her house, the Flower Pot). And so 1995 ended, we had moved from deep despair to a feeling of hope.

Now I'll start on 1996; I'm quite impatient to get these memories finished and to read all about them!!

1996

On 1st January 1996 I note in my diary that we sang 'Auld Lang Syne' in church. I think that is quite unusual.

Anyway, browsing through my diary I conclude that 1996 was a good year in many ways.

In January Christine Jordis arrived from Paris to compose a page-long article about David for *Le Monde.* She arrived for supper on January 11th, looking as radiant as ever. She then amusingly interviewed David with a tape-recorder until Liz came to fetch her at 10 pm

They got on very well and the next day Liz arrived with Christine for another interview. My French group carried on in the dining room. Then after lunch we had to say a fond farewell. A few weeks later the article came out in Le Monde with a good photograph by Mark Gerson. I enjoyed making my French adult classes translate Christine's beautiful French in *Le Monde.*

I gave several talks called 'New Year Resolutions', which I much enjoyed because it made me feel that resolutions were really worthwhile. Also in January Sue and I went to the Quay Arts celebration for getting over £1 million for improvement to the building. It was a very happy event, but I fear there have been difficult repercussions during the year of 1998 at the Quay Arts. Its such a unique place, and we all love it. David has given two poetry readings in the New Theatre, along with some fellow poets, and we also had his eighty-second birthday party there in the Rope Store while launching his new book, *Selected Prose 1934-1996,* published by Enitharmon on October 10th 1998.

But, back to 1996! Early in February Marion came down to look after David while I went to Zoe and Peter's wedding in Cheltenham. Kevin, Jean and Grace drove me to it, and again it was good to be at a family wedding. Although Sheena and Kevin had finished their marriage a few years ago, it was nevertheless a happy family affair. Zoe looked so beautiful coming down the aisle on Kevin's arm. We all went to a very pleasant hotel for the reception, and I was so pleased to meet up with Sheena and her new husband, and my two grandsons, Oliver and Seth. Zoe was so affectionate towards me, although we don't see each other much these days. She is a school-teacher and they say she is very like me in many ways. We stayed away for a night and came back via Oxford to lunch with Jenny. Marion had coped very well with David. It is wonderful that I can get away sometimes.

Also in February, Andy the gas-man fitted a fire in the sitting room. This completely changed my life work-wise. I had always sworn that as long as I could move I would always have a 'real' fire, but the work it entailed was intolerable really. Now, thanks to modern science, at the flick of a switch 'real' flames spout up in a moment. I imagine that this was the biggest and best idea that I ever had to lighten my load from the drudgery of housework. It was as well because I see that in March Alan came again to stay. Peter Baldwin also came for David's signature on 150 books he is publishing — David's translation of Pierre Jean Jouve°s essay *The Present Greatness of Mozart,* first printed in 1940. Andrew Zackwieky from America came; he is quite a faithful fan. Bertrand Rouby and Arno He'din, two French fans, visited as well. I love having them all but wish I could entertain as well as I used to.

On April 4th 1956 we all arrived on the Island to live in Yarmouth, so of course I made it an excuse for a fortieth celebration party. Luckily it was just warm enough for the garden. Kath made one of her lovely cakes, and all the family, including Jenny from Oxford and Zoe and Peter from wherever they live now; plus a scattering of friends like Matt and Denise, and Mark and Anne G. We videoed quite a lot of the party. Poor May, aged eighty-nine, tripped and cut her leg and had to be taken to hospital. Michael came on his own, and Kevin made one of his lovely funny speeches. Forty years on the Isle of Wight was an anniversary worth celebrating.

We'd hardly got over that when it was time for Miles and Sue to celebrate their twenty-fifth wedding anniversary. As always, when they organise anything, it is done on a most professional and generous scale. I have a glow of pride recalling their wedding, and the way they have managed to sustain their marriage in such a balanced way.

Nothing daunted, our WI celebrated its seventieth birthday with a really delicious lunch party at our good WI Hall. Looking back, 1996 seemed to be full of celebrations! Kevin was fifty on 16th June, so we had a tremendous party at Holmfield, so well organized. Kevin was in fine form playing with all the children. He is wonderful with children. I rose to my feet to record his birth and first fifty years. There was one celebration after another in 1996, and I was able to leave David to attend them all.

But on June 27th, it was David's turn to have a big celebration. The French Government had honoured him by making him a *Chevalier dans l'Ordre National des Arts et Lettres.* So off to London we went. It took a lot of organising beforehand. We were allowed to send out fifty invitations which took a lot of deciding. Then there was the slight crisis over what to wear. To our consternation the Simpson Suit which David wore to the Palace in 1992 was too small. Days of lying in bed and no exercise had made David's waist expand! So, at the very last minute, the owner of Osbornes arrived with a selection of smart blazcrs, trousers and shirts, and the day before we left we had it all fixed up. I was pleased to be able to wear the Pierre Cardin long colourful dress which Mary had found for me in an Oxfam shop in Newport. So all was well. We had hired a wheelchair from the Red Cross, which Kevin handled very well. Sue looked after me and we were at the French Institute at 3.30 pm. There, Monsieur Lacombe greeted us with tea and croissants, and showed us the enormous hamper of goodies that had arrived from Fortnum & Masons. It was yet another of Simon Callow's generous gestures.

By 6 pm the room was arranged for the presentation and all our guests had arrived. Monsieur Poivre d'Avour spoke fulsomely about David and all he had done for France over the years. Then he pinned on a most elegant medal with the traditional kisses. Mark Gerson was there to photograph it all, and my kind Sue stuck to her video camera for the whole event. David replied in good French, then he was persuaded to read two of his French translations. Much clapping and toasting with champagne followed. The food was delicious too and I was busy taking people to have a word with David. Kathleen Raine sat on the sofa with him. Philip Marsh was there in a wheelchair. Of all the events in my twenty-four years with David, this one gave me the most pleasure. Stephen Stuart-Smith of Enitharmon had arranged the publication of David's verse translations that very day, so he was busy selling signed copies.

At about 8 pm Kevin started us on the journey back to catch the Portsmouth ferry. On the car radio we heard the announcement of David's award on the BBC programme *Kaleidoscope.* This was a pleasant surprise. We stopped for a quick snack and caught the 10 pm ferry. Truly a day of great rejoicing! The next day Sue had a big family party for Emma's twenty-seventh birthday, so we watched the video of David's presentation all together.

On June 30th Brenda Ross came down to unveil a garden seat at Calbourne in memory of Steve. All her family came to support her and it was followed by a service in the church. Caroline Ross spoke most movingly about her father and his connection with the Island. We then all met up at the Calbourne pub, and I gave Lesley a lift back for the last ferry. On July 1st Michael Wishart died and his friend Tim and his family all rang. He will be missed.

All through July David watched the tour de France. It amazes me how much he enjoys it. Len continued to worry about Kit, so weak in hospital. She rallied a little to hear about David's award, but very sadly she died on 15th July. Len was with her all through the night. He bravely made all the funeral arrangements himself. It must have been a terrible ordeal for him, and we have become close friends ever since.

It was very warm in July 1996. Sue took me to a wonderful concert in the grounds of Osborne House, followed by fireworks. About 3,000 people had all taken picnics. Sue brought champagne and salmon. It was better than Glynebourne!

Also, Sue took Marion and me to lunch at the Royal Corinthian Yacht Club during Cowes Week. We saw the Britannia for the last time. When it is fine weather Cowes Week can be quite special. David had new spectacles from Willets, and the golden frames make him look quite different.

Sean Street and Julian May came down on August 9th to make a programme about David and his views on translation. As always with those two it was a very happy day. The resulting programme on Radio 3, *The Cartographer of Thought,* was good too. David read his translations very well. Roger Howe from Cork came to interview David for the day. Also Michael Sweeney who is trying to write Roland Penrose's biography. Quite a task. David is very patient with all the biography writers. He has known so many people and they like to get anecdotes about them.

On September 17th David's broadcast was on Radio 3. It was good and several people rang up when it was over, which gave us a nice feeling. Having made a decision that David's eightieth birthday should be celebrated, I went full steam ahead to get it organised. Liz willingly agreed to hold it at the Flower Pot, and Mr Ireland said he would do the catering. Jake made the very intriguing invitations, and all the guests accepted. It was a warm and sunny October day on the 10th. We had quite a party for lunch; Tony Rudolf, Peter Baldwin, and Alan. They all came laden with good cheer. Stephen arranged to fetch the ninety-three year old Edward Upward, and Gareth Beaumont drove us to the party so that I could drink plenty of wine! Liz was ready for us and, as we arrived, eighty red roses arrived with a great message from Simon Callow. It went with a swing after that. The caterers made it so easy for me. After Kath's delicious chocolate cake, Tony Rudolf proposed David's health in a most flamboyant way, and David responded. The party ended with the grand-children swimming in Liz's indoor pool, and Kevin splashing in with them. Liz played all David's favourite music on the piano. Sue managed to video it all, so I love watching it when friends come to see themselves at the party. David had some wonderful presents, and everyone was so good to him. I felt happy that it had gone well. It was hard to believe that he had reached the grand old age of eighty, in spite of his frail health. Radio Solent, Radio 3 and the Telegraph all mentioned it in their news! And that was nearly the last celebration for 1996.

Except that Roger Scott came down from Newcastle for three days in November. He helped us tidy up and sort through lots of books. He had nearly completed editing all David's prose which he wants to publish with Stephen Stuart-Smith next year. This will be a wonderful collection and we will be in his debt for ever.

1997

The year started with a complete re-vamp of the kitchen by Babs and Peter. This was a great success and I was able to buy a new gas cooker that I really liked, and a huge fridge-freezer. It made January go quite quickly. Also, the Queen was disposed" to increase David's pension by another £250 a year as they put it, in a letter from Downing Street.

Very sadly my good friend Muriel Hind died from a stroke in January, and she was such an asset at our French classes.

Sue started me off at a creative writing class at St Mary's Hospital. We went all day on Saturday for a month, and it was great.

Another excitement was the gift of a washing machine for my seventy-fifth birthday on 1st February. I had always said that I didn't need one, but really this was the best family gift I've ever had. And as everyone always says, 'I can't think how I ever managed without!'

With that and the gas fire, I should have had time for everything, but the arthritis in my knees was getting steadily worse. Social Services came to the rescue by lending me several useful aids.

In February we had great celebrations at the WI Hall. The whole movement started one-hundred years ago in Canada. Also the Trinity Theatre in Cowes was a hundred years old, so Dorothy Bentham and I enjoyed a very good concert there narrated by Cyril Amey.

On Sunday, February 23rd, Kevin drove us to Bath for David to read at their Literary Festival. This went much better than I expected. Julie came with us. It was good to meet up with George and Olga Lawrence again. Also many old friends had made the long journey. David did very well and we have the recording to prove it! At the end of February, Sue and I heard that we had passed our creative writing course, and the presentations and a party would be in April.

On March 1st we had a visit from Matthew Thomas, a charming young man who is writing a book about the Poets of the 1930s who frequented the Soho pubs. He is also a photographer and he took an excellent photograph of David which Stephen chose for the back of the dust jacket of the *Selected Prose* published in 1998.

Reading through the first six months of my 1997 diary, I note we had friends down to see us many times, which was good because travelling is such a big undertaking now. As a member of the Healing Arts Committee I was invited to the unveiling of a colourful 'koan', which was installed at the entrance to St Mary's Hospital. I had to be in a wheelchair for this because it entailed a lot of standing about, and a party afterwards. Harriet Kline, the poet in residence for Healing Arts, looked after me. We had a pleasant lunch with all the VIPs who had come down from London for the occasion. It was also on televised. Most Island people thought the koan was a waste of money, and there was endless correspondence about it in the local paper. Now, in 1999, they are still moaning about it. I find it sad that people get worried about such trivial things. Our old friend Julie Lawson, from the Arts Committee, came down with the maker of the koan, Lilane Lijn, and I enjoyed a laugh with her. It was an early Easter, and I collected £70 for my sponsored slim for Tear Fund. We managed the usual egg hunt in the garden too. It was a beautifully warm and sunny March 1997.

On May 1st, Matt came to tea telling us he would go back to America if the Tories won again. David and I managed to hobble to the Polling Booth and vote for the lady Labour Candidate. I was fairly hopeful that Tony Blair would lead the Labour Party to victory, but I thought by a small margin.

Imagine how thrilled we were when all through the night our bedroom television and the radio boomed out all the Labour gains, and the sweeping majority for Tony Blair. I was glued to the set all day.

Anthony Minghella's film *The English Patient* won seven Oscars, so we all felt very proud of him. There was a special charity showing of it at the Medina Theatre where our Island boy was honoured.

Also the new theatre at the Quay Arts was opened and named after him. I was very pleased when they asked if David would give a reading there on National Poetry Day, October 9th. It was the opening night of the theatre, and Nicholas Johnson had lined up a prestigious number of poets to read with him. Iain Sinclair, Aidan Dun, Barry Mac Sweeney and Nicholas Johnson. It was well organised and attended, and written up most fulsomely on David's Internet page. The next day was David's eighty-first birthday, so we celebrated with Roger Scott, Stephen Stuart-Smith and Alan Clodd, with a lunch party at home. In the evening we had a supper party too with Sue, Liz and Annie Goosens.

On 11th October 1997 Gordon Bowker and his partner came to see David with a view to writing his biography. They have been down twice since, so I hope it comes off one day. It is a gigantic task and must be far worse than an autobiography! I'm getting on quite fast with mine now, and long for it to be finished!

A really world-shattering event happened on August 31st 1997. We heard on the World Service in the night that Princess Diana's car had been in a bad crash in Paris. She was leaving the Ritz Hotel with Dodi Fayed, El Fayed's son, and the news was bad. All the media television covered this sad new for many days. It was a tragic loss of a beautiful young life, and we all felt sorry for her two sons. The Queen came down from Balmoral to pay her a special tribute on television. The funeral was on September 6th, and we were all glued to our television sets. It was very well organised and the service in Westminster Abbey beautifully arranged. Diana's brother, Earl Spencer, gave a most moving account of her life, and pledged us all to remember her with love and he hoped the media madness would spare her sons. London was crowded out, and a sea of flowers spread outside Buckingham Palace and her own home. Personally, I'm glad we all paid Diana so much love and respect. We didn't give her much of it in her lifetime, and I was pleased to be with David to share that very moving time.

An anthology of poems written out of mental distress came out in 1997 called 'Beyond Bedlam' and included three by David. It was published by Anvil Press, and edited by Ken Smith and Matthew Sweeney. All the royalties were dedicated to the Mental Health Foundation and the MIND Campaign. It was well illustrated and it was brought out to mark the 750th anniversary of the founding of Bedlam Hospital.

Richard Hallward brought our copies down, and we liked him so much. We keep in touch and he threatens to tell our story on television, but I take all that with a pinch of salt, as they say! I recall that he and I had very bad backs when he came for the day!

Sadly, in 1997, Jean and Kevin split up for good. This was a shame because they were such good friends, but like his father Kevin finds fidelity an impossibility. When I feel too smug about how wonderful my children are, it is good to realise that they are not perfect, as none of us are. All the same these family break-ups do cause a lot of misery and they affect so many people.

The year ended quite well with Jenny down for a pre-Chistmas frolic, and the usual quota of family fun and WI celebrations.

I note in my diary that I made a resolution to see Dr Stainer about my very painful arthritic knees and legs but, apart from painkillers, he wasn't optimistic about treatment. I guess I must learn to live with it. I did go to Sue's Boxing Day hockey match, and for the first time in forty years I wasn't even able to bully off or play, but I much enjoyed the huge crowd that were there for tea and 'Trivial Pursuits' afterward. It was good to see my godson, Jono Carver with his four children. Also Louise with her two, and Christine and John Carver. A real gathering of the clans. Christmas as it should be, thanks to Sue and Miles.

1997

1998

Now I'm starting on almost the last year of my memoirs. It is hard to sort out the trivia from the important. I shall have to take it all as it comes. I find it very hard to get things into the right order, and it is difficult not to be repetitious! But today, April 25th 1999, I feel quite elated that I am on the last leg, as it were, of my seventy-seven years of memories.

My dear friend Jean Harrison, who had been coming on and off for French lessons for many years, took it into her head to take her GCSE via the Technical College. Imagine how delighted we all were when the result was an 'A' grade. Sue took me off to see the Royal Shakespeare Company performing *Romeo and Juliet,* and that was a joy to us both. On Sunday 3rd May, Simon Callow came for lunch and Jenny came to help me. Simon was in high spirits, bringing a bottle of champagne, and keeping us laughing until after tea, when he disappeared in a taxi to finish off his Orson Welles book which he was writing, under pressure from his agent at Seaview.

May was a really warm and sunny month. Sue made good preparations for her fiftieth birthday party on the 6th. We all met at the Wellow Institute for a big sit-down feast, and dancing to her favourite Irish Group. I felt so proud of her and all my family. Liz drove me to the party, which was a help. I just about managed the conga, but my knees were so painful, and I had twisted my ankle!

For the WI that month I had to pretend to be the President for a members' meeting, and then we had quite an amusing musical quiz, which I enjoyed organising. I finished by reading the prose I had written called "The Man in my Life" for a WI National competition! Needless to say it was all about meeting David. I didn't win a prize, but I'm glad I attempted it!

Carole (French), David's cousin, arrived on the Island for David's concert at the Quay Arts. It was good to see her again. She stayed at the George in Yarmouth.

Aidan Dun had arranged this reading, for himself and David. Another Carole had worked really hard to make it all go smoothly. We met on an extremely hot night at the Quay Arts. Aidan was magnificent in a white costume, moving in time to his poetry and playing the guitar. His grandmother, Marie Rambert, would have been so proud of him.

As arranged, David read his moving *Miserere* sequence of poems which made a splendid contrast. We all had drinks at the Quay Arts afterwards.

The next day we celebrated our twenty-third wedding anniversary, and that was fun. We had it all out in the garden. Sue, Liz and Emma did all the work.

Alan, Roger and Stephen came; also Aidan and Carole and Roger Howe. It was all over about 6 pm and it had been a wonderful few days. I was really sorry that Carole wasn't able to stay for the party, but she left us some lovely things for it.

Sean Street rang to say that Simon Callow had rushed back from Los Angeles to record David's 1930s surrealist film script, called *A Procession to the Private Sector*. Sean came over on the 19th to record David being interviewed, and reading the poem he wrote at the same time to accompany the script.

Amidst all the excitement of May, Tony Astbury came to stay with us. He slept in Toad Hall and enjoyed it. He wants me to choose my twenty favourite poems for publishing in the year 2000. We've known him for over twenty years now, and he is always promoting poetry readings at his school in Warwick where he teaches.

Ron Stocker did some very hard work with our boxes of books on the landing. He is another faithful and kind friend. Before I die I would really love to have all David's books sorted out and on bookshelves. I must really want that enough to organize someone to do it for us.

On May 30th Neville Braybrooke invited us to his seventy-fifth birthday party. As it was such a special occasion David was persuaded to come too, and he managed it without a wheelchair. It was a real literary lunch with Edward Upward, the ninety-five year old writer; Francis King, Isabel Quigley and others. Francis King proposed Neville's health, and he made a most elegant response, ending up by reading a poem which he had written that morning. We then all had champagne and cake. Victoria, Neville's step-daughter and her two daughters, provided us with a delicious salmon lunch.

Poor Annie Goosens was seriously ill in hospital during June, requiring an emergency operation.

Will Stone called for the day on June 3rd, all the way from Suffolk.

Conrad, Marjorie and Tim came for lunch on June 7th. Kevin prepared and cooked it all. Then I sat in the garden with Tim. It's a shame that he is going deaf, but he copes with his blindness very well. I feel I have an affinity with him. Conrad is getting over his stroke quite well.

James Clements, a nice twelve-year-old, started coming for English and his mother was most appreciative.

June was cold until the 20th, when I set out with Sue to stay with Ben and Joan at Marlow. It was arranged because Dial Close School, where I started teaching in 1940, were holding their first reunion. Marion Fletcher kindly agreed to look after David for four days, so we were up and away. It was a lovely break from routine, and meeting all my old pupils again after fifty-eight years gave me quite a thrill. I think it was because of this reunion that I decided to start on my memoirs.

Apart from that find spell of hot weather at Marlow, the rest of the summer was a bit of a washout.

In July, Ellen von Kessell and a Paris TV journalist arrived for a few days. They interviewed David on camera about Humphrey Jennings, and they had me talking on camera in the garden and reading David's poetry. They stayed at a B&B in Cowes. We enjoyed their visit and they were generous guests. Ellen still keeps in touch from Paris. She is teaching at the Sorbonne now.

Also in July, Sue took me over to the Cheshire Home. They were giving a thank-you party to all the helpers. The Cheshire Homes were started by Leonard Cheshire fifty years ago, and we were also invited to an excellent 'do' at St. Paul's Cathedral in September with Basil Hume in charge. It was a very moving service and I was proud to be part of it. It is so good that Sue agrees to drive me anywhere, and we have had lots of fun together.

The biggest event for David in 1998 was the publication of his *Selected Prose 1934 - 1996*. These prose pieces had been hunted down and superbly edited by Roger Scott. He also wrote a preface to the book, and there is an introduction by Kathleen Raine. Enitharmon Press, under the guidance of Stephen Stuart-Smith, were the publishers. David was really pleased with the whole production. It was a lovely idea to launch it on his eighty-second birthday at the Rope Store of the Quay Arts Centre. We turned it into a celebration party. Dear Neville proposed David's health, and praised the book. Even at the high cost of £30 it has been selling steadily ever since, and there have been some good reviews.

Roger Scott came all the way down to stay. He missed the actual party, but we had quite a good supper with champagne. Liz and Sue joined us and helped so much.

I started on another creative writing class with Sue at the Quay Arts. John Goodwin took us on, and thought up some quite inspiring situations to write about but, on the whole, I have decided that I'm not really a born writer!

On November 23rd 1998, Alan Munton came for the day to interview David about his early life and poems. I think he intends to write a paper about David for his University. We enjoyed his visit.

For the last two years I have enjoyed teaching French to Lottie Smythers. I don't think that in all my sixty years of teaching I have found such a delightful pupil. She doesn't go to school because of her IQ, and she is as beautiful as she is clever. Her accent is quite amazing too. Now that I am so crippled, she helps me go for a swim after each lesson, so it is a really happy arrangement. I hope life is good to her, and I am grateful to Mike Izard for suggesting the job to me.

1998 ended quite well. Jenny came to stay for Christmas, which was a special treat, and we all had Boxing Day with Sue, except for my poor David who finds getting out to parties too much of an ordeal.

Now that I have completed my task, I will have to close these memoirs.

1999

1999 has been good so far, especially our trip to London to read for Nicholas Johnson at the Diorama Theatre. All our very dear friends came to listen to David. It was on March 14th, which was also Mothering Sunday, so I had Kevin and Sue looking after us all day. The guest list was quite auspicious at the theatre too. I think David found the long car drive a bit uncomfortable, and the feeding arrangements were not good either. But, on the whole, he was very stoic about it all and Nicholas paid us very handsomely.

Pat Clayton, who is typing these memoirs for me, has also typed a novella by David from the 1930s called *April,* which we hope will be published in the year 2,000, edited by Roger Scott.

Another very good thing happened in December 1998, David's cousin Carole, with her husband Harry, came to live at Chawton Barn next to Northwood Church.

This has been a boon for us, and they arranged a great New Year's Eve lunch here for us. Although we don't see each other as often as I would like, it is good to know she is only half a mile away and we always meet on Sundays in church.

NOW FOR THE SUMMING UP OF MY LIFE SO FAR!!

Seventy-seven should be a very lucky age, but so far it is nothing very special.

I find my slowed-down life frustrating at times, but on the other hand, there are so many compensations, like being waited on by everybody, and being able to park on double yellows anywhere, and the feeling that I can self-indulge without feeling guilty.

I would like to make a long list of thanks-yous to the people who have given me such a full life, but that is impractical so, for the moment, *I'm closing down!!!!*

     *   *   *   *

1999

A Continuation

I've been reading over *My Love Affair with Life* which ended on the eve of 2000. It seems that I felt that life would soon be over and nothing else of interest would happen for us. But I was wrong, so now, for my own interest, I'm starting on a sequel with possibly no definite end? I'm hoping it may cure a fit of the blues which I've been having lately. So off we go on October 23rd 2001 for an exploration of life in the 21st century!

This was a happy day because Sue took me to the big cinema complex in Newport to see a film called *Enigma.* I wanted to see this because my special boyfriend, Kevin O'Neill, was sent to Bletchley Park in the 2nd World War to decipher the Enigma codes, which were fiendishly difficult. He was sent there because I told Billy Stephenson how wonderful he was. Billy was more or less in charge of the Secret Service, and Kevin O'Neill said it was because of me that he landed up at Bletchley Park. It was good to watch the film and to be in a real cinema again with a huge screen. Sue took me in our new wheelchair, so it was all done in great style. At last, I feel that I am on the mend from the big operation that I undertook in July of 2001. The idea of having a knee replacement had been hanging over me for about four years. I heard so many conflicting reports, mostly that it was superbly successful, so that when my name came up on the waiting list I decided to try my luck.

The family were amazingly supportive, and Sue made up rotas so that David would be looked after while I was in Hospital. When the actual day came, I was more excited than frightened. Sue made a splendid Job of taking me to Hospital and settling me into Luccombe Ward. I had a nice end-bed with only six other ladies in the ward. We watched the men's finals at Wimbledon; then we went to call on Neville Braybrooke in a nearby ward. He was just out of intensive care, and recovering from a major operation for bowel cancer. He was his usual charming and humorous self, and we spent a happy hour with him and Victoria.

Finally it was time for Sue to go, but not before a most reassuring Doctor had come to discuss what sort of anaesthetic I would like for the operation on the morrow. The fact that he was tall, blonde, German, and very attractive, helped a great deal, and I agreed to all his plans. Sue knew him from parties where they had met.

I found the night a bit long, mostly because of endless trips to the loo and the general hospital noises. But the night Sister was very sympathetic. No breakfast was allowed and a student nurse helped me into quite a pretty operating gown. Sharp at 8.30 am two cheerful porters wheeled me into the operating theatre. For about half-an-hour, a very pretty lady held my hand,

and we both chatted about our lives. It was quite soothing, and soon there appeared the delectable doctor, and off we went to have some anaesthetic put into my backbone. This wasn't painful and he was very reassuring. Quite regretfully I hardly remember being wheeled in to see Mr Nazra for the 2-hour knee replacement. The next thing was being woken by Dr Hoff, and I asked him who was going to get David's breakfast! After about an hour of drowsiness, I was back in the ward. It was quite a treat when Diana, our local curate, called with a lovely card and prayers and good wishes. The student nurse rang to tell David that the operation was over, and he was pleased.

I had to lie back on low pillows all day, and I didn't get, or feel like, any food. The morphia machine arrived, and when the pain was bad I had to press a button. As I expected instant relief (which didn't come), I pressed again, and I was soon rather bewildered! In fact, I was convinced I had moved wards and was in some Isolation Hospital! But I managed to keep fairly sane when Warren and Jake, with Margaret King, called with flowers and pressies. In fact all the family came for those two bewildering days, and the flowers were lovely. On the third day, I was back to a sort of normality, with no catheter or morphia machine, and most of the tubes out. So I didn't have to carry my bag of urine everywhere, I did have one nasty hiccup with it, while waiting three hours for an X-Ray. I was glad when that was over. In the meantime, I obeyed the 'physio terrorists' as they are called, and did my painful exercises of knee-bending. The machine for that was very efficient. I had it for three hours at a time, and it was easy. Trips on the commode to the loo were far less worrying than I expected!

My dear friend Mary arrived with Keith, and lots of delightful things and good cheer! I was really touched by the amount of visitors who kept arriving. Sometimes it was tiring to find them all chairs. The nurses don't help out when you feel exhausted. There is no limit on time or numbers! But I did enjoy a good laugh and prayer with Graham, our charming young vicar. All the time I tried to keep up with my huge diary, and a tape for Jenny.

While writing this, it occurs to me it might be better to turn this bit of my memoirs into a new talk. I shall call it 'My Knee Job', and try to make it amusing for the many people who go through much the same thing. So to continue my Hospital write-up, which only lasted eight days, though I feel I could write a book about it.

My X-Rays pleased Mr Nazra, and he told me I could go home providing I could satisfy Mrs Bell, the Physiotherapist. I did, just, and she taught me to use elbow crutches instead of the Zimmer. They have a horror that we will become fat and lazy. This is a distinct possibility, bearing in mind that the meals were excellent and well thought out. The endless cups of tea and chat were helpful, and mounds of fruit and chocolate were always on my table. It was a bit like celebrating a birthday every day, and being lazily in bed for it. But, a very sad day came for me on July 14th. The Sister drew the curtains around my bed and told me that Neville Braybrooke, one of our very best friends, had died early that morning. I shed quite a few tears then. Victoria called in to see me after that. Neville was so special, and we are missing him dreadfully. I still think of him as still here and wish I could ring him for Saturday tea. Victoria is so courageous when I ring her, which is not often enough.

So back to the Hospital and quite a weepy Saturday. I did get a 'phone to ring David, who hadn't heard, so we had a good talk. Many visitors called, and we had a rest from Physio for the weekend. I did, however, go to the Chapel Service in a wheelchair. It was very pleasant, but I found it hard to sit still through the sermon because of pain. I was disappointed that there were only ten of us. And so the days in Hospital were over and it was time to organize the home-going. As always, Sue rose to the occasion and took all my accumulated things back home, so that I could have a clear run on the actual day.

Emma, the student nurse, helped me with a shower. She nearly took out my stitches due to a misunderstanding with the Sister. Thankfully I stopped her, because if I had let her do it I would have been in Hospital for another two weeks.

At last it was time to say goodbye to all the Staff, and leave behind a few pressies. I dressed and was taken down to the disposal lounge to await the ambulance. It was quite fun being driven home in a fully-equipped ambulance in a wheelchair. However, when I arrived home I had to manipulate the slippery slope on my crutches, and so back into the arms of Sue and to see David again.

It was strange to be home again and, after sitting downstairs for a bit, I was longing to go up to my own bed. The room looked so lovely with flowers, and it was all tidy. Sue quickly persuaded me to stay in bed for tea and supper, so I felt happy and spoilt, but annoyed that I felt so tired and weak. I won't go into day-by-day details of my convalescence, because it is all in my diary. Its over three months since the operation, and I confess that I'm disappointed that my walking is slow and painful, and the nights still uncomfortable. I wish all the people who told me about their knee-jobs had been more truthful.

Today as I write, October 25th, I'm waiting at 1015 am to talk to Dr Stainer because David seems to be quite ill and in pain. When Dr Stainer arrived in his usual attractive and efficient way, he gave David a thorough examination, and even managed to take some blood. Then he decided that it was probably a painful attack of diverticulitis, so pills were prescribed and Emma fetched them. A great relief that it wasn't cancer. But the days and nights are painful for David, so we must adjust to that.

2000

Now I want to recall the year 2000. It started so well with our new kitten, Bobby, given to us from Bradleys at Chawton Farm on New Year's Eve, and making himself so much at home. New Year's Eve itself was well celebrated from every country on television, and David and I loved that. Even far into the night when we shared the television upstairs in my bedroom. Also, as a special start to New Year's Day, Graham our Vicar, invited me to read Tennyson's tribute to the New Year in church. That pleased me very much. The year passed swiftly. I enjoyed my pupils for French, and young ones for reading and spelling. It's something that I can do however crippled I am.

On the 1st May 2000, Jenny had a farewell lunch with us all before departing for Mongolia. We were all so proud of her. I was a bit anxious, selfishly wondering how I would manage without her. Somehow, it wasn't as bad as I had expected. We kept in touch by 'phone and with letters. I really enjoyed writing to Jenny, once a week, and telling her all the news. Writing letters has always been a joy to me. I now cope with all David's because with his increasing blindness, and shaking hand, apart from signing his name (on the many cheques I present to him) he can hardly write or read at all.

I would like to touch on our Silver Wedding celebrations on 17th May 2000. Yet another day that I thought we would never reach. Because of this I made quite a few plans beforehand. Milo made the attractive invitations on his computer, with a little 'photo of us on it. We decided to book the Salty Sea Dog restaurant because of its pleasant venue and quite good food. They said they could only manage fifty of us for a sit-down buffet, so that made for some careful thought. To our pleasure, everyone accepted. Even Christine Wild in London and Colin Benford from Peterborough, David's bibliographer. Neville agreed to propose our health. Most of my large family was ready and willing to help as usual. The day dawned sunny and windy. We were really touched by the deluge of cards and charming Interflora's which arrived. One very special one from Edward Upward gave us great pleasure. At ninety-five he was virtually the guest of honour. Miles brought him over from Sandown and Kevin lifted him home. Kevin also drove us to the event. The car was laden with memorabilia that Christine Wild arranged with an expert touch. Having been an exhibitionist at the Festival Hall, it was in good hands! When we arrived (later than we thought), the room was filled with guests and wine and laughter. David was in a wheelchair but looking very elegant, and my Pierre Cardin dress came to the fore (God bless Mary Woodger for finding it for me).

When all the feasting was over Neville made one of his great speeches for us. It was good to recall the one he made on our wedding day, when forty of us crowded into our little sitting room.

I responded to Neville's words and greeting, and thanked the guests. Then I tried to make a few funny remarks about marriage, and the best way to make it work! I suggested that husbands should listen more to their wives, however boring, and sympathise wholeheartedly; also to be willing to sign any cheque when asked! It went down quite well.

It was soon all over, and we were driven home for our daily rest. Christine Wild called for tea, and implored me to 'Let go more' and 'stop trying to be so perfect!! Excellent advice.

And so a special day ended with our usual smoked-salmon and white wine, with Vienetta ice cream for supper!

That was the really big event for us in the year 2000. The rest was frequently token up with visits to the Hospital for my stupid arthritis, and many of my family supporting me through Bell's Palsy which I didn't enjoy at all.

Pam Winsor helped me through all that illness and all the other little dramas most willingly, and so did Mark. The garden, as always, was a tremendous joy to me, and we managed quite a few meals outside. Mostly only for teas, because David finds moving about slow and tedious.

2001 November

I take up my pen again, after three weeks of worry over David. Following an alarming fall during the night, Wightcare came to lift him back onto his bed with an electric gadget, and it went quite smoothly. He looked so ill and pale that I called Dr Stainer, who agreed that I could no longer give David sufficient physical support, so the wheels were set in motion for a Nursing Home. I was frankly amazed by the speed and efficiency of the enterprise.

Gill Thomas arrived to fix up a bed at Inglefield in Totland Bay. She also arranged for the lady manager and a male nurse to come over and talk to David. Hardly had that finished when the ambulance arrived, and I just had time to throw a few things together.

The paramedics and Jenny had quite a job to get David onto the Stairlift, and so off at 5 pm to Totland. Jenny and I both had a little weep as the ambulance drew away. It was all a bit alarming. However, we settled down for the evening and Jenny produced a good supper and saw me to bed. She then went off back to look after Warren, Sue's house and animals. What a girl!

I rang the Home next day to hear that David was very confused, but settling in. Jenny went to see him and to take needful things. I eventually went to visit him the next day. David looked very ill and immobile, but at least he knew who I was.

And so the weeks passed. Miraculously he became much better. Now today, as I write on 22nd November, we are making plans for his return tomorrow.

Once more on the date of the 23rd, which has always meant so much to us.

And now it has all changed? My 'wonderful' Social Services have not been able to find any help for us, so David has to stay at Inglefield. I hope he is not too disappointed. I am.

However, Susie came at 4 pm to cheer me and have tea, and whisk me off to see Amélie, a good French film. It managed to take my mind off the dreary plans for the future. Back home. Sue made us delicious scrambled eggs, and then went to a meeting at the Hospital. I went slowly, and rather sadly to bed on a very cold night.

2002 January

Now that I've nearly finished all my letters, I think its time to recall my thoughts about David's death on November 25th 2001 at St Mary's Hospital at 8.30 pm. I find it hard to start on this but I want to. So it was at 9 am on November 25th 2001 when Inglefield Nursing Home rang to say that David was being sent to A&E at St Mary's, due to a very bad night. So Jenny and I had a big change of plan. First to tell Sue we couldn't come to lunch, and then to drive off to St Mary's. Our timing was quite good; David arrived almost as soon as we did. He looked very pale and his breathing was bad. He didn't like using the oxygen mask because, with it on, he couldn't speak or drink. The African doctor was clearly very worried and agitated. He asked me endless questions and had a nurse to help him. After two or three hours they decided to take David to the new Medical Centre. He was to be more fully examined before going to a ward. While they were doing that, Jenny and I shamelessly ate a real Sunday lunch in the Hospital canteen. Back to sit with David and talk a little. A sympathetic male nurse was very helpful, and we talked to a doctor. I had a strong feeling that David was in a very bad way. However, we were advised to go home for a little while at 4 o'clock, so we did. Very soon the Hospital rang again asking us to come back soon. Dear Jenny drove me in the dark to the Hospital. It was such a help having her with me.

So from 5 pm until 7pm I sat holding David's hand and talking to him. He spoke of Paris and asked me to ring Christine Jordis. He discussed the Christopher Robin poems with a helpful young nurse.

Finally, a bed was ready for David in Newport Ward. It was a long way to get to it, so Jenny pushed me in a wheelchair. A huge men's ward at the top of the Hospital came into sight, and David was given the end bed with the curtains drawn around us. A nurse persuaded me to ask David to drink some chalky stuff which he did reluctantly. Through the curtains I could hear husbands moaning to their patient wives.

Emma arrived in her lovely sympathetic way, and we had a little giggle over the oxygen mask. Poor David was breathing in such an exhausting manner. I realised he couldn't continue for long like that. In fact, I prayed that he would finally pass away into a peaceful state.

While I was praying, his breathing gently became calm, and then all was silent. I gave him a kiss and called the nurse. There was a sympathetic feeling from everyone. Jenny was most efficient in gathering up all our things, and driving me and Emma home. Jenny soothingly brought me supper in bed, and I was able to sleep eventually.

Early on Monday morning I rang Stephen Stuart-Smith to tell him the sad news. He listened quickly and sympathetically and offered to take on a great deal of work for me. He told the media, and the news of David's death was on all the BBC radio news bulletins. It was strange to hear it! Later, Stephen took on the arduous task of tackling the solicitors about David's will, and organising the newspapers who all published very fulsome obituaries about David. All this quite helped the sad shock of David's death. My family was quite amazing, quickly coping with it all, and yet letting me do whatever I felt in need of doing.

One of the most pleasant times was when Graham Morris came round to discuss the funeral service. As always Graham struck exactly the right note, and in no time we had organised something that I was sure would have pleased David.

Stephen asked if he could give the funeral address, which was a great load off my nrind. The rest of the planning just fell into place. On the service sheet Graham had printed David's poem 'Lines', and also a word of thanks from me and an invitation for everybody to come back home after the service.

The next thing to be sorted out was the arrangement with Lloyds the Undertakers. This was taken on most efficiently by Tony Packer, and it wasn't half as much of an ordeal as I had feared.

During the week leading up to the funeral, the family sorted out the garage, garden and the muddles in all the rooms of our tiny house, while I coped with many 'phone calls and letters that came pouring in. They were a great help.

Sooner than I expected David's funeral day was with us. I was surprised by the amount of friends who rang saying they were coming. The day passed in a bit of a daze. All four children and Liz, Rose and Poppy worked hard to get the after-funeral party ready. Exactly at 11.50 am, after we'd had a glass of champagne organised by Kevin, the big black stretch limo arrived for us, and off we all went to be met by Graham and Diana and a few latecomers! Emma had to shush us when we were all chattering outside the Church! Then came David's huge coffin with my little spray of coloured flowers on top. We took our seats, Graham recited David's poem 'Lines' as the coffin was carried in.

Then Graham welcomed us and the service began. The church was very quiet and still. Stephen gave the most awe-inspiring address, beautifully delivered, and Kevin followed with 'Apologia'. I read 'Crossing the Bar' and Jenny sang 'Fear no more the heat of the Sun' beautifully. Then it was prayers and hymns, which were sung quite lustily for a funeral service. It was all over quite soon, and David's coffin was carried out of the Church with Graham reciting Wordsworth's 'Hymn to Immortality', which was most appropriate. Dear Diana went with the coffin to the Crematorium to see the service through to the end.

I sat in my wheelchair in the porch and greeted the enormous number of guests, while the family scuttled back to prepare the feast.

By the time I arrived most of the guests were there. I was most touched by the flowers which were brought back to the house afterwards. I settled myself on the sofa and one by one friends came to sit beside me. Gordon, Mick Mares, all the Wilds, Sebastian Barker and so many more! Stephen was much praised for his oration. He had to leave promptly to sign something for the solicitor. By about 4 pm everyone had left. Jenny insisted I had a little kip upstairs. When I went down again, dear Miles was there having a snack. He hadn't been able to be at the reception because of work. He gently inspected my broken tooth and said he could easily fix it one day at the surgery.

The funeral, which was a big ordeal, was over! I had so many good letters of thanks too. The rest of the days and weeks consisted of trying to make sense out of the solicitors, who weren't too satisfactory, paying the big bills and arranging direct debits. Kevin and Milo were most diligent about everything.

I started on my thank-you letters, and counted up to one-hundred-and-fifty condolence cards. Christmas came and went with much joy, except for the wretched 'fluey' colds and coughs that affected everyone over and over again. I had a few weeps, but as I write now on 25th January, I feel much stronger.

The weather has been typical for the end of January. Terrible gales and torrential rain. I'm pleased that I've started swimming again; I go with Nick and Chris and it is really easy. I hope it will improve my mobility.

Also, all my pupils are back, and I find that stimulating. I've enjoyed listening to A Burning Sound and Processions to the Private Sector on Radio 4, and I've plenty of BBC tapes to send on. Sean Street has been so kind and helpful - he was the BBC Producer. Church was good with Graham today, and my precious Jenny cheered me up at lunchtime, and Emma at tea time.

I would like to add now a few words about Bobby, our cat, and his reaction to David's death. Bobby didn't like to see so many people in the garage, garden and house at David's funeral party. Especially as there were so many men. He's always been anti visitors. Anyway, he ran off and there was no sign of him for two days. Eventually, I spotted him in the garden, limping with his paw held in the air. Michael came over to help, but felt that trying to catch and restrain him would do more harm than good, so we left it at that. Then for nearly a month, Bobby refused to come into the house, so I left his favourite food outside the front door. It was frosty and very cold, so I worried about him. I had to be very patient and then very slowly and gradually he came back inside the outhouse to eat.

Then, one happy day at the very end of January, Bobby came in the front door early. A big break through was when he drank milk from my cereal bowl, after inspecting David's bed. Now he purrs and stays with me for most of the time! Also the frogs, which have been threatened by a terrible virus, have laid spawn and two of them seem quite well, thanks be to Mark.

I have been giving talks lately called 'Bearing up to Bereavement', and I have found it therapeutic.

Also I went to London with Sue for the launching of 'The Book of Sand', a selection of David's poems with illustrations by Agathe Sorel. Timothy West read poems from it.

My next trip was to Marlow to attend my brother Edward's funeral. This was quite uplifting and I'm so glad I went to it.

The next excitement may be Paris in November for the second launching of 'The Book of Sand - Le Livre du Sable'.

It's almost impossible to draw an autobiography to an end.

But I shall stop writing today on August 17th 2002 , with the hope that Jenny and Sue might finish it, after I've left this very interesting world, which — on the whole — has made me very happy.

Judy Gascoyne, August 2002

Address for David Gascoyne's funeral
by Stephen Stuart-Smith

You couldn't possibly invent a life-story like David Gascoyne's. Not even the most fanciful of scriptwriters could devise such a heady mixture of drama, celebrity, romance, and survival — survival against all the odds.

The elements are familiar to you all: the musically-gifted child singing the services at Salisbury; the teenage poet and novelist astonishing his contemporaries by his assurance and originality; the English voice of the Surrealists, through his translations and his *Short Survey;* co-organiser of the 1936 Surrealist exhibition; broadcaster in Barcelona for the Republican cause in the Spanish Civil War. Already the story is remarkable, yet by this point, of course, David Gascoyne was only 21. His reputation was already established, as was his passion for French culture and his contacts with some of the legendary artistic figures of the time — André Breton, Max Ernst and Salvador Dalí among them.

Then, in the war years, publication of his *Poems 1937-1942,* a collection in which he set aside his Surrealist mask and emerged as one of the greatest religious poets of the century. The lover of the metaphysical poets, especially George Herbert and Henry Vaughan, found his own idiom and created something utterly memorable with it, reflecting the insecurity of an individual in the midst of unimaginable suffering.

The next stage in the story, from the early 1940s to the late 1950s, encompasses wartime acting, the return to Paris, where he was expelled from the Surrealist movement, the bleak post-war years in which writing, once a compulsion, became more of a curse. Yet out of these years of apparent silence grew *A Vagrant* and then in 1956 the radio poem *Night Thoughts* — significant achievements by any standards. Then in the mid-1960s, his return to England after a decade in France. He settled for a time with his parents, then in institutional care, latterly at Whitecroft hospital on the island.

And it's at Whitecroft that the final chapter — the astonishing final chapter — begins, when a volunteer worker reads a poem, *September Sun,* to the inmates, and finds to her amazement that she is reading to the poet himself. The meeting of David Gascoyne and Judy Lewis has to be one of the most extraordinary in literary history. No less extraordinary was their marriage, which was to lead to David's recovery, his return to writing, and to him travelling the world, with Judy at his side, as an elder statesman of the international poetry community, fêted everywhere as one of the most distinguished literary figures of the century, and a focus, back here in Northwood, for scholars, broadcasters, writers and fans from all over the world. In 1996 the French government gave him one of its highest cultural decorations — an honour he would never have sought, but which brought him intense satisfaction.

Judy's love and support sustained him for almost thirty years: her greatness of heart, her sociability, her love of travel and adventure, her home-making, made David's last years a fitting and richly-earned coda, and all of us today would wish to pay tribute to her. Judy's children, too, having acquired a stepfather both unexpected and unorthodox, were wonderfully kind to him.

In the past twenty years almost all of David's writings have come back into print, or have been published for the first time - poems, translations, journals, and a massive volume of *Selected Prose* written over sixty years, which dazzled reviewers by its richness and variety. I can think of no one who has been able to write with such authority and intellectual power about Symbolism and Existentialism, Dada and Surrealism, Romanticism and Neo-Romanticism, and quite a few other -isms, and about such a vast range of writers and artists, from those before his time — Novalis, Hölderiin, Carlyle, van Gogh — to those he knew personally, often as lifelong friends. The English cast includes his closest friends George Barker, Kathleen Raine, Lawrence Durrell, Antonia White, Roland Penrose, and the painter Julian Trevelyan, and widens to include his wartime editor Tambimuttu, the American poets Kenneth Patchen and Lawrence Ferlinghetti, and a host of French luminaries, from Louis Aragon and René Char to Benjamin Fondane and the poet who commanded David's deepest respect and affection: Pierre Jean Jouve.

David had a formidably well-stocked mind and one of the keenest of intellects. Conversations with him were both a delight and a danger — a delight in that his conversation was spellbinding; a danger only in that few visitors could match the depth of his knowledge and the richness of his reminiscences. Certainly his publisher was hard-pressed to keep up. His memory was crystal clear, his observations brilliant, his stories sometimes implausible but always true. And of course it was part of his modesty and courtesy that he assumed you understood every reference, every aside. David was never boastful, never name-dropped to impress, and he was a rarity among great writers, in always being interested in the person he was talking to. A conversation with him was an interchange of views, not a monologue. To the end, his curiosity about literature, the visual arts, music and current affairs was undiminished.

And though his Journals and his two novels are shot through by intense introspection, at the same time he had a kindly concern for others and an overwhelming desire for the good of humanity. To read the poems he wrote on the eve and in the early stages of the Second World War is to recognize a mind scarred by the gruesome prospect of man's inhumanity to man. *But poets,* he wrote, *make beauty out of ghastliness,* and how triumphantly he was to do that, not least in *Miserere* and his metaphysical poems.

There was humour, too albeit as dry as a French Sançerre. And he didn't lack the common touch. It might come as a surprise to some of you, when you think of the aristocratic Mr Gascoyne, the student of Kierkegaard and Heidegger, to know that he was a devotee of *Coronation Street* — though perhaps its appeal was primarily to the ex-Surrealist.

A few of you will have known him in his early manhood — the years in which his matinée idol looks must have turned many heads. On his eighty-fifth birthday it was joy to hear him reminiscing with his friend Anne Goossens of taking her to dance clubs in Paris in the thirties. For most of us the enduring image will be of an older man, either on a public stage, when the beauty and drama of his delivery could be mesmerizing, or at his home in Northwood — the elegant and erudite raconteur, welcoming, gracious, dapper. (Dapper indeed: his collection of ties must be the largest outside the costume department at the V&A.)

And although silences and depressions could descend on him, sometimes to the bewilderment of visitors, he remained wonderful company. Seated in his chair in Northwood, surrounded by books, letters, papers, the inevitable box of chocolates, he was strategically placed to see not only the television, but also the many arrivals and departures of those who sought him out for what he had achieved and for what he represented: an unwavering commitment to the life of the poet, in an age which needs poetry more than ever before. In his modesty he would be astonished to see how many of us have come to pay homage to him and to witness his own departure. Yet in fact he was rich in friendships, and his work touched many lives, as it will continue to do long into the future. David's elegy on Paul Eluard is strikingly appropriate for his own funeral: *Words spoken by one man awake in a sleeping crowd / Remain with their unique vibration's still breathing enigma / When the crowd has dispersed and the poet who spoke has gone home.*

Judy has been deluged with tributes to David in the past week, but she hasn't yet heard these extracts from letters I've received in the last few days. I'd like to share them with you. The first, from the poet and academic Jeremy Hooker, begins: *I know you will be grieved by David Gascoyne's death, and I am writing to express my condolences. He is a major poet — there is no past tense in these matters — a poet rare in modem England: anguished, ecstatic, prophetic. His work will be known and valued when that of many currently more acclaimed poets is not.*

The second is from David's dearest and oldest friend, Kathleen Raine. She writes *You understand my woe at David's return to the world he really belonged to, for he was more angelic than human and never really belonged here.* [He was...] *the last great poet.*

On the day before David Gascoyne died I was in the newly reorganised 20th century rooms at the National Portrait Gallery. The magnificent bust of David by Gertrude Hermes, made in 1956, the year of *Night Thoughts,* has now been placed so that it faces not inwards to the visitors, but out of the gallery windows. It looked to me rather like the figurehead of a ship, the eyes looking up to the clearest and bluest of November skies. Its placement wasn't exactly an omen, but in retrospect it seems symbolic of his going, of the liberation of death, an exploration of other worlds. It brought to mind his poem *Tenebrae,* of 1937, which is so characteristic in its use of the imagery of day and night, light and dark, but with one uncharacteristic touch: an ending which seems to glow with optimism for the future, for the beyond:

The Bronze of David by Gertrude Hermes, 1956, in the National Portrait Gallery

Tenebrae

Brown darkness on the gazing face
In the cavern of candlelight reflects
The passing of the immaterial world in the deep eyes.

The granite organ in the crypt
Resounds with rising thunder through the blood,
With daylight song, unearthly song that floods
The brain with bursting suns:
Yet it is night.

It is the endless night, whose every star
Is in the spirit like the snow of dawn,
Whse meteors are the brilliance of summer,
And whose wind and rain
Are all the halcyon freshness of the valley rivers,
Where the swans,
White, white in the light of dream,
Still dip their heads.

Clear night!
He has no need of candles who can see
A longer, more celestial day than ours.

David Gascoyne, 1937